COOKING BY THE DOZEN

COOKING BY THE DOZEN

Elizabeth Pomeroy

Hamlyn

London · New York · Sydney · Toronto

I would like to thank Mary E. Widdicombe B.A. Hons
(London), Senior Tutor at our school, for her interest and help in
putting this book together.

Photography by James Jackson
Line illustrations by Sheelagh Bowie

First published in 1984 by The Hamlyn Publishing Group Limited
London · New York · Sydney · Toronto
Astronaut House, Feltham, Middlesex, England

ISBN 0 600 32404 4

Set in Monophoto Bembo by Tameside Filmsetting Ltd.
Printed in Spain

CONTENTS

USEFUL FACTS AND FIGURES

Notes on metrication

In this book quantities are given in metric and Imperial measures. Exact conversion from Imperial to metric measures does not usually give very convenient working quantities and so the metric measures have been rounded off into units of 25 grams. The table below shows the recommended equivalents.

Ounces	Approx g to nearest whole figure	Recommended conversion to nearest unit of 25
1	28	25
2	57	50
3	85	75
4	113	100
5	142	150
6	170	175
7	198	200
8	227	225
9	255	250
10	283	275
11	312	300
12	340	350
13	368	375
14	396	400
15	425	425
16 (1 lb)	454	450
17	482	475
18	510	500
19	539	550
20 (1¼ lb)	567	575

Note: When converting quantities over 20 oz first add the appropriate figures in the centre column, then adjust to the nearest unit of 25. As a general guide, 1 kg (1000 g) equals 2.2 lb or about 2 lb 3 oz. This method of conversion gives good results in nearly all cases, although in certain pastry and cake recipes a more accurate conversion is necessary to produce a balanced recipe.

Liquid measures The millilitre has been used in this book and the following table gives a few examples.

Imperial	Approx ml to nearest whole figure	Recommended ml
¼ pint	142	150 ml
½ pint	283	300 ml
¾ pint	425	450 ml
1 pint	567	600 ml
1½ pints	851	900 ml
1¾ pints	992	1000 ml (1 litre)

Spoon measures All spoon measures given in this book are level unless otherwise stated.

Can sizes At present, cans are marked with the exact (usually to the nearest whole number) metric equivalent of the Imperial weight of the contents, so we have followed this practice when giving can sizes.

Oven temperatures

The table below gives recommended equivalents.

	°C	°F	Gas Mark
Very cool	110	225	¼
	120	250	½
Cool	140	275	1
	150	300	2
Moderate	160	325	3
	180	350	4
Moderately hot	190	375	5
	200	400	6
Hot	220	425	7
	230	450	8
Very hot	240	475	9

Note: When making any of the recipes in this book, only follow one set of measures as they are not interchangeable.

INTRODUCTION

This book is written for those who have, on the whole, only catered for average-sized family groups – say four to eight – and who want to be able to cook confidently for larger numbers. It is aimed at those who want to know how to cope with cooking for family celebrations, holiday guests or charity functions and also for those who would like to join the professionals in directors' dining rooms, public relations parties, small hotels, restaurants and clubs where they may have to cater for forty-eight or more.

There are practical tips for the enthusiastic amateur on equipping the kitchen and adapting cooking techniques and recipes for larger quantities. These recipes are designed to be practical, interesting and a pleasure to make.

Current textbooks for trainee chefs going into large-scale commercial catering are factual, but tend to discourage rather than inspire those who want to carry the standards of good home cooking into a wider field. This means making use of modern equipment and techniques without sacrificing the traditional skills which produce tasty, attractive and wholesome food to the menacing gods of speed and profit. In the long run it is doubtful whether a restaurateur who subjects his customers to menus produced by low-paid staff from factory flavoured soups and sauces and portion-controlled packets of tasteless processed fish and meat will increase or even retain their custom for very long.

The French maintain that food should be cooked with love and certainly if the cook does not enjoy preparing the meal and looks on it as a dreary chore, the unfortunate recipients will find that eating it is equally dreary. When the atmosphere in the kitchen is not of fearful foreboding or fatalistic calm, but rather one of confident and lively anticipation, then everyone will enjoy it.

Adapting the Kitchen for Larger Numbers

If the extent of your cooking for a crowd is limited to the occasional wedding reception or celebration party you can usually borrow fridge, freezer and even oven space from a friend or neighbour but most home kitchens need certain modifications in order to cope comfortably and efficiently with larger scale cookery on a regular basis. The extent of this will depend on the frequency and scope of the meals required and the type of equipment already installed.

In order to save time and energy when making larger quantities of food a variety of inexpensive items of electrical equipment are available. These can be bought as accessories to your existing mixer or as independent units. You might consider a peeler for potatoes and root vegetables, a grater-cum-chopper for such foods as cheese, nuts and parsley and a blender for making soups, sauces and purées. For baking you will need a mixer for whisking eggs, creaming cakes and mixing pastry dough. The dough hook attachment, for kneading yeast dough, is a great time saver.

There are several good food processors on the market now. They may seem expensive, but they are handy for as well as mixing they will chop, slice, mince, grate and chip. However, processors do not whisk egg whites successfully. A processor with a continuous flow facility saves emptying the bowl between batches.

It is important to have enough free work top space with an adjacent electric point available so that electrical equipment can be kept out permanently. If the machine must be extracted from a cupboard or drawer every time it is needed, it will probably spend more time in the cupboard than in use.

Equipping the Kitchen

Cookers

An electric cooker with a fan-assisted oven is ideal for batch cooking. The heat is circulated at the same temperature over the whole oven so that you can bake, for instance, eight pastry flan cases or roast four chickens simultaneously instead of in relays.

A useful extension to a fuel storage cooker like an Aga is an electric hot plate with two or more burners which can be plugged into a point without extra installation charges.

Another useful auxiliary is a warming oven in which to heat plates or keep prepared food warm while other dishes are finished off in a quick oven.

A microwave cooker is excellent for defrosting frozen food and reheating cooked dishes.

Cold storage

You may find that you need extra larder space for storing larger quantities of raw ingredients, you may need more refrigerator space for dishes cooked in advance or that freezer space for prepared stocks and sauces, pastry or frozen vegetables is too limited. One way of increasing freezer space is to reduce surplus stock by boiling it down before freezing it. You can replace the water content when you defrost it. Be sure to label the containers appropriately.

If you already have a large freezer, an extra larder-refrigerator without a freezing compartment gives more cold storage space than the standard model.

Ventilation

Good ventilation in the kitchen is as important as an adequate supply of hot water. An extractor fan which can also be reversed to draw in cool air is best.

Hot water supply

If this is variable an auxiliary sink heater which only takes up a little space in the kitchen but supplies instant hot water may be a good investment.

Lighting

Strip lighting is good in one respect because it doesn't cast any shadows, however some tubes bleach the colour out of food and should be avoided. Strategically placed spotlights can be very useful.

Pots and pans

When choosing large pans remember that they are heavy to lift and carry especially when filled. A stock pot is very useful and can also be used for cooking a whole ham.

A fish kettle with a grid is useful for cooking a whole salmon but a large roasting tin can also be used. It will take a large fish placed diagonally or 2–3 salmon trout, wrapped in foil, which can be poached very successfully in the oven.

A large roasting tin with 2.5 cm–/1 in of water in the bottom can be used as a bain-marie. It is just as efficient at keeping sauces warm as a purpose-made bain-marie.

A thermostatic deep fryer not only prevents any risk of overheating the fat but, if it has an inner container which filters the fat and a cover with a replaceable filter, the frying smells will be greatly reduced.

Sauté pans are preferable to deep saucepans for making sauces and sauté dishes such as Calf's liver and marsala sauce (see page 83).

Flameproof casseroles which can be used on the top of the stove to brown meat and vegetables before adding liquid are more useful than ovenproof pottery. There are many attractive designs which can be put directly onto the dining table saving cooking and washing up time.

Adapting Cooking Techniques

Timing

Correct timing is important to the home cook but vital to the professional who is cooking for clients who are expecting and paying for their meal to be delivered on time. Working against the clock is stressful. However, there are some simple rules which make life easier. The first thing to remember is the naval maxim – 'prior planning prevents poor performance' – so if the menu, marketing and cooking schedule is planned, the rest of the work should go smoothly. The experienced cook will have little trouble in planning the schedule, but there could be pitfalls for the less experienced.

It is not unlike planning a railway time-table. First, establish the hour at which each train has to arrive at its destination, next at what rate it travels and lastly at what time it has to start so that it will arrive safely on time without any dire collisions or delays en route. For train read dish and if your problem is assessing the preparation and cooking time of the individual dishes, make a note of this on each recipe the first time you make it and remember that cooking is like any other craft – skill and speed are the rewards of practice.

Vegetables

It is often a shock to someone accustomed to catering for say, six people, to find out how much longer it takes just to wash, peel and chop vegetables or fruit for 12, unless you have some of the electrical equipment described earlier.

It is obvious that you will need large saucepans but at first you may not realise how much longer it takes to bring them to cooking temperature compared with ones half the size.

For green vegetables, pasta and rice, which have to be plunged into boiling water, filling the pan from the hot tap will speed up the operation, but the introduction of cold food will lower the temperature and it will take several minutes to come back to the boil.

Eggs

If you are hard-boiling two or three dozen eggs at a time, it is a good idea to use a blanching or frying basket so that they can be easily submerged and lifted out and the simmering time accurately monitored.

Chilling Food

The temperature of the refrigerator and freezer will be raised when you fill the shelves with dishes which require chilling or freezing and a margin of time must be allowed for this. Large birds and joints of meat will clearly require longer to cook and cool completely than small, but it may not be so obvious that a double-sized crème caramel will need considerably longer in the oven to set and also longer to chill in the refrigerator. Ices and frozen desserts will freeze much quicker in shallow containers and individual moulds than in larger, deep containers.

Sauces

When making a large quantity of sauce with a flour and butter base, you may shorten the cooking time by heating the milk or stock in a pan while making the roux in another pan. When cooked, cover the sauce with damp greaseproof paper to prevent a skin from forming. Cover closely and keep warm in a bain-marie.

When cooking butter and egg based sauces, like a hollandaise, over simmering water, use a heatproof glass or metal bowl rather than a plastic one which would slow down the thickening. When the sauce is ready keep it warm in a bain-marie. If these sauces are left over direct heat they will separate. These and cold sauces made with oil, like mayonnaise, are rapidly and successfully made in a food processor if the makers' instructions are followed carefully.

Frying

It is difficult to do shallow frying in large quantities on a standard sized cooker. It is more economical both in terms of space and time to use the oven instead. Fish and chicken joints can be coated with beaten egg and breadcrumbs and cooked in roasting tins with a little fat – this is sometimes called oven-frying.

Deep frying is made much easier by using a thermostatically controlled deep fryer.

Adapting recipes

When adapting a recipe for six servings to twelve, it is not always advisable simply to double the quantity of all the ingredients, especially spices or aromatic herbs.

If, for example, your soup recipe for six allows a

margin of one cup, it would be increased to a surplus of 700 ml (1¼ pints) over 24 portions, this is not very economical. On the other hand, when using a recipe for a casserole which says 'add sufficient liquid to cover the meat', you will often find when serving that there is too little sauce for 12 or more portions. The shape of the casserole and the meat will be affected by Archimedes' principle and may lead you astray. You will need to allow a generous 1.5 litres (2½ pints) of sauce for every 12 portions. Even though less would cover the meat in the casserole, when served out, each portion will need about 125 ml (4 fl oz).

The liquid in soups and sauces is liable to evaporate during cooking and, if they have a roux base (butter and flour), they will also thicken during chilling and freezing. You will, therefore, need to add extra stock, water or milk when reheating.

Number and Size of Portions

When catering for 12–48 persons it is easier to calculate quantities and to avoid food looking institutionalised if pies, flans, gratins, puddings and cold desserts are presented in units of six or eight portions. It will also facilitate rapid serving which is important for hot food. In addition it is less wasteful as any remaining surplus is more likely to be left as an appetising dish rather than messy, unattractive debris on a large dish.

Garnishing

It is a useful aid to serving equal-sized portions if the garnish or decoration is arranged with this in view. For instance, on a savoury flan for six people if you place six mushrooms or bacon rolls equally spaced around the edge so you can cut between them, or on a trifle for eight people, rosettes of cream can be piped in a pattern which indicates the eight equal portions.

When the final garnishing has to be put on hot food immediately prior to serving, it is a good idea to select, prepare and arrange it in advance on a board or tray so it can be whipped on to the dishes at lightening speed and still look elegant and appetising. This will save you from any last minute rush.

Menu Planning

The correct composition of the menu is as important as the perfection of the cooking, for dishes delicious in themselves, served in a badly composed menu, can result in a horrid meal.

Menu planning requires judgement and imagination and until you gain experience, there are certain guidelines which you can follow.

Guiding Principles

1 Establish the type of occasion for which the meal is required. Is it a formal or informal affair? What time of day is the meal for?
2 Take account of the funds available, consider whether they are lavish, average or restricted.
3 Use seasonal foods which are of good quality and good value.
4 Have regard for the known or probable tastes of the guests. Avoid serving food without giving an alternative if there is any likelihood of it being unacceptable on religious grounds. For instance, do not serve pork for Muslims or Jews.
5 Select dishes which will suit the season. However, even when it is hot include some non-stodgy hot dishes unless a cold buffet has specifically been asked for.
6 Consider the type and number of dishes on the menu in relation to:
  a the skill and speed of the cook
  b the equipment and the space in the kitchen – type of cooker, size of refrigerator and freezer
  c what help, if any is available, for preparing and serving the meal
  d the time available for shopping, cooking, serving and cleaning up

Choice of Dishes

1 To give variety to the menu alternate the colour, flavour and texture of succeeding courses including the garnish and vegetables which accompany the dishes. For a one-off occasion a particular colour scheme might be requested. For instance, I was entertained in Paris one summer to a *dîner rose*. The ladies were asked to wear rose coloured dresses and the gentlemen rose coloured button holes. The table linen was two-tone rose pink and the table decoration roses in various shades of pink. The menu was:

Crevettes roses (large pink prawns)

Borshch (Russian beetroot soup)

Sole Walewska (sole garnished with lobster and pink coral sauce)

Suprême de volaille au paprika (Chicken breasts in paprika sauce)

Strawberry bombe and Raspberry soufflé

Wines: Vin Rosé and Pink Champagne

It was all delicious but we did feel rather be-pinked at the end. On leaving each lady was presented with an exquisite rose and rose-scented perfume, with the host lamenting that it was not a string of pink pearls!

2 Do not combine hearty family dishes with haute cuisine dishes in the same menu. Keep the menu on one plane.

3 Beware of serving a highly flavoured first course like kipper pâté if the following dish is light and delicate.

4 Take care not to serve a sauced vegetable with a sauced entrée.

5 It is usually convenient to include on the menu one or more dishes which can be partly or completely prepared in advance, such as soups, sauces, pastry and meringue cases, savoury mousses and cold desserts.

SUGGESTED MENUS

SUMMER

Wedding Buffet

Salmon Mousse or Dressed Crab

*

Chicken Véronique

Avocado, Tomato and Cucumber Salad

*

Savarin with Strawberries

WINTER

Wedding Buffet

Cucumber and Green Pea Soup

*

Blanquette of Veal

Glazed Carrots

Rice with Fresh Herbs

*

Apricot Charlotte Russe

SUMMER

WINTER

Coming of Age Party

Gazpacho Andaluz

＊

Apricot and Honey Barbecued
Chicken

Coleslaw

＊

Old-Fashioned English Trifle

Coming of Age Party

Mushroom Puffs

＊

Toulouse-style Cassoulet

Green Salad

＊

Gâteau St. Honoré

Dinner Party

Lombardy Terrine

＊

Turbot Dugléré

Casseroled Courgettes

Creamed Potatoes

＊

Hazelnut Galette with Peaches

Dinner Party

Bisque of Shellfish

＊

Lamb Cutlets in Pastry

Brussels Sprouts with Chestnuts

Château-style New Potatoes

＊

Orange Cup Puddings or
Raspberry Parfait

HORS D'OEUVRES

These are meant to be appetisers and should be served in small portions. They must always be selected with the subsequent courses in mind. For instance, don't choose a fishy hors d'oeuvre if a fish course is to follow, and avoid a rich, creamy appetiser if the following dishes have the same texture and ingredients. Many of the hot hors d'oeuvres are interchangeable with the little savouries served at the end of dinner.

FLORIDA FRUIT COCKTAIL

ILLUSTRATED ON PAGES 46–7

This is particularly delicious in spring and summer when fresh herbs are available.
You can vary the fruit, you could use oranges instead of melon, or grapefruit
segments instead of pears and you could substitute grapefruit juice for the lemon.

No. of servings	6	12	24	48
cucumber	100 g/4 oz	200 g/7 oz	400 g/14 oz	800 g/1¾ lb
tomatoes	150 g/5 oz	300 g/11 oz	600 g/1 lb 6 oz	1.2 kg/2¼ lb
melon	4400 g/14 oz	800 g/1¾ lb	1.6 kg/3½ lb	3.2 kg/7 lb
pears	120 g/5 oz	240 g/8 oz	480 g/1 lb 1 oz	960 g/2 lb
DRESSING				
lemon juice	2 tablespoons	4 tablespoons	120 ml/4 fl oz	240 ml/8 fl oz
sunflower oil	4 tablespoons	120 ml/4 fl oz	240 ml/8 fl oz	480 ml/16 fl oz
salt	½ teaspoon	1 teaspoon	2 teaspoons	4 teaspoons
freshly ground black pepper	to taste	to taste	to taste	to taste
caster sugar	2 teaspoons	4 teaspoons	2½ tablespoons	5 tablespoons
tarragon, chopped fresh	1 tablespoon	2 tablespoons	4 tablespoons	8 tablespoons
dried	1 teaspoon	2 teaspoons	4 teaspoons	8 teaspoons
chives, chopped fresh	2 teaspoons	4 teaspoons	2 tablespoons	4 tablespoons
dried	1 teaspoon	2 teaspoons	4 teaspoons	8 teaspoons

Place all the dressing ingredients in a large screw-top jar and shake them up.

Slice the unpeeled cucumber fairly thickly and quarter the slices. Skin the tomatoes, remove the cores and seeds and place over a sieve to extract the juice. Cut the flesh into wedges and add to the cucumber.

Cut the melon into 6 or 8 (400-g/14-oz) portions according to size. Place the seeds in a sieve with a bowl under it to catch any juice. Cut the flesh off the rind with a grapefruit knife and cut it into bite-sized pieces. Mix with the other fruit. Add the juices to the dressing.

Peel and core the pears and cut them into small chunks. Mix all the fruit together in a bowl.

Shake up the dressing and adjust the seasoning. Pour over the fruit and toss everything together. The dressing must cover the fruit to prevent any discolouration. Chill well.

Mix again before serving. Place in individual glass coupes. Put some of the tomato on top to make the coupes look attractive.

ICED FRUIT CURRY

This is a mild Malayan style fruit curry which can be served as a first course or it can be an accompaniment to a main dish of cold duck or chicken. The fruit can be varied according to the season. In summer use fresh apricots, peaches and melon and in autumn pears, plums and greengages. In winter plumped dried apricots, peaches, canned mangoes, pineapple and tangerines.

No. of servings	6	12	24	48
desiccated coconut	2 tablespoons	4 tablespoons	50 g/2 oz	100 g/4 oz
boiling water	200 ml/7 fl oz	400 ml/14 fl oz	800 ml/1¼ pints	1.5 litres/2¾ pints
butter or margarine	75 g/3 oz	150 g/5 oz	300 g/11 oz	600 g/1¼ lb
onion, finely sliced	100 g/4 oz	200 g/7 oz	400 g/14 oz	800 g/1¾ lb
flour	75 g/3 oz	150 g/5 oz	300 g/11 oz	600 g/1¼ lb
curry powder	1 tablespoon	1½ tablespoons	3 tablespoons	6 tablespoons
curry paste	2 teaspoons	1 tablespoon	2 tablespoons	3½ tablespoons
coriander seeds, crushed	2 teaspoons	1 tablespoon	2 tablespoons	4 tablespoons
preserved ginger, chopped	2 pieces	4 pieces	8 pieces	16 pieces
chicken stock	900 ml/1½ pints	1.8 litres/3 pints	3.5 litres/6 pints	7 litres/12 pints
prepared fruit, see above	675 g/1½ lb	1.35 kg/2¾ lb	2.7 kg/3¾ lb	5.4 kg/12 lb
double cream	100 ml/3½ fl oz	200 ml/7 fl oz	400 ml/14 fl oz	800 ml/1½ pints
lemon juice	2 tablespoons	4 tablespoons	100 ml/3½ fl oz	200 ml/7 fl oz
salt	to taste	to taste	to taste	to taste
duck, about 2½ kg/5½ lb, roasted	1	2	4	8

Infuse the coconut in the boiling water until required. Melt the butter and fry the onions lightly in it. Over a low heat, stir in the flour, curry powder, curry paste and coriander. Cook gently for 5 minutes, add the ginger, strain the coconut liquid and add it together with the stock, simmer for 30 minutes.

Peel, core or halve and stone the fruit. Cut into neat pieces and mix into the sauce and add the cream. Sharpen with lemon juice and add salt to taste. Chill thoroughly. Carve the duck and take the flesh off the bones. Cut into neat pieces and add to the sauce.

Serve with fluffy rice and fried poppadums.

MUSHROOMS WITH HAZELNUTS

ILLUSTRATED ON PAGE 155

The grilled hazelnuts make a delicious topping to this dish. Make sure you use small flat mushrooms, not button mushrooms.

No. of servings	6	12	24	48
hazelnuts	60 g/2 oz	120 g/4½ oz	240 g/8½ oz	475 g/1 lb 1 oz
mushrooms, small flats	450 g/1 lb	900 g/2 lb	1.8 kg/4 lb	3.6 kg/8 lb
butter, softened	150 g/5 oz	300 g/11 oz	600 g/1¼ lb	1.2 kg/2¼ lb
lemon rind, grated	1 teaspoon	2 teaspoons	4 teaspoons	3 tablespoons
garlic cloves, crushed	3	5	10	20
parsley, chopped	2 tablespoons	4 tablespoons	50 g/2 oz	100 g/4 oz
salt and pepper	to taste	to taste	to taste	to taste

Toast the hazelnuts under the grill and rub off the skins with a dry cloth. Coarsely chop them. Trim the mushroom stalks and either wipe the caps, or rinse and dry them. Cream the butter and mix in the grated lemon rind, garlic and parsley. Season to taste with salt and freshly ground black pepper. If unsalted butter is used, a little extra salt will be needed. Melt the garlic butter in a sauté pan, put in the mushrooms, cover closely and cook gently for 5–10 minutes, until the mushrooms are softened and the butter is absorbed. Shake the pan from time to time.

Arrange the mushrooms in a single layer in individual gratin dishes, darkside uppermost and sprinkle with the chopped hazelnuts. Flash under the grill to finish. Serve with hot, crusty French bread.

NOTE: *The hazelnuts, mushrooms and garlic butter may be prepared in advance so that the final cooking can be done quickly. When cooking for large numbers never sauté more than 450 g/1 lb of mushrooms in a pan at a time.*

—————— VARIATION ——————

For a slightly richer dish, add a little white wine to the sauté pan.

Avocado, Cucumber and Tomato Salad (see page 145)
and Salmon Mousse (see page 28)

*Chicken Véronique (see page 112) and Savarin Au
Rhum (see page 170)*

Cheese, Apple and Ham Quiche

ILLUSTRATED ON PAGE 88

This is a very versatile and inexpensive recipe. Evaporated milk is a very good, cheap substitute for real cream. For vegetarians the ham may be omitted and you will still have a tasty filling. This dish can be served hot or cold. It can be made in advance and reheated, or frozen and then defrosted.

No. of servings	6	12	24	48
shortcrust flan case 20–23 cm/8–9 in	1	2	4	8
butter or margarine	40 g/1½ oz	80 g/3 oz	150 g/5 oz	300 g/11 oz
apples, chopped	350 g/12 oz	700 g/1½ lb	1.4 kg/3 lb	2.8 kg/6 lb
onions, chopped	50 g/2 oz	100 g/4 oz	200 g/7 oz	400 g/14 oz
ham trimmings, or streaky bacon, chopped	75 g/3 oz	150 g/5 oz	300 g/11 oz	600 g/1¼ lb
evaporated milk or cream	300 ml/½ pint	600 ml/1 pint	1.2 litres/2¼ pints	2.4 litres/4¼ pints
cheese, grated	75 g/3 oz	150 g/5 oz	300 g/11 oz	600 g/1¼ lb
eggs, beaten	1	2	4	8
paprika	to taste	to taste	to taste	to taste
salt and freshly ground black pepper	to taste	to taste	to taste	to taste

GARNISH *small bacon rolls and a few apple slices; parsley sprigs or watercress, if serving cold*

Set the oven at moderately hot (190 c, 375 f, gas 5). Line a flan ring with pastry and bake blind. Melt the butter, fry the apples lightly in it and spread them over the base of the flan case. Fry the onion and ham in the same butter until golden. Add the evaporated milk and heat to scalding point, but do not boil. Remove from the heat and mix in the cheese, stir until melted. If the flavour is too mild, add some more cheese. When the cheese has melted, mix in butter, the eggs and season to taste with paprika, salt and freshly ground black pepper. Pour the mixture over the apples. Place in the heated oven and bake for 20 minutes or until the filling is set.

Serve hot garnished with bacon rolls and a few apple slices; if serving cold garnish with sprigs of parsley or watercress.

GNOCCHI WITH SMOKED HAM

This is a warming and satisfying first course, ideal for hungry skiers. The raw smoked ham gives these gnocchi their special flavour. The Westphalian type is less expensive than the Italian prosciutto, but is equally tasty. Dry Cheddar cheese can be used instead of Parmesan in the mixture, but the traditional Parmesan is best for the topping.

No. of servings	6	12	24	48
milk	1 litre/1¾ pints	2 litres/3½ pints	4 litres/7 pints	8 litres/14 pints
semolina	150 g/5 oz	300 g/11 oz	600 g/1 lb 6 oz	1.2 kg/2½ lb
butter	15 g/½ oz	30 g/1 oz	60 g/2 oz	120 g/4½ oz
Cheddar or Parmesan, grated	75 g/3 oz	150 g/5 oz	300 g/11 oz	600 g/1 lb 6 oz
Prosciutto or Westphalian ham, finely chopped	120 g/4½ oz	240 g/8½ oz	480 g/1 lb 1 oz	960 g/2 lb 2 oz
egg yolks, beaten	2	4	8	16
ground nutmeg	¼ teaspoon	½ teaspoon	1 teaspoon	2 teaspoons
salt and freshly ground black pepper	to taste	to taste	to taste	to taste
TOPPING				
butter, melted	60 g/2 oz	120 g/4 oz	240 g/8 oz	480 g/1 lb 1 oz
Parmesan, grated	50 g/2 oz	100 g/4 oz	200 g/7 oz	400 g/14 oz

As gnocchi mixture is very thick and is apt to stick to the pan, it is best not to cook it in batches larger than for 12 portions.

Bring the milk to the boil. Sprinkle in the semolina, stirring steadily. Cook gently, still stirring until the mixture is stiff enough to support a wooden spoon standing upright. Remove from the heat and mix in the butter and the cheese. When the cheese has melted, gradually stir in the chopped ham and then the eggs. Season to taste with nutmeg and freshly ground black pepper. You may need to add a bit of salt but do this sparingly as the ham will be salty.

Oil a Swiss roll tin(s) and using a palette knife dipped in cold water, spread the mixture out in it to a thickness of about 1.5 cm/½ in. The large size of Swiss roll tin, 33.5 cm × 23 cm/13 × 9 in will make 6 portions. Chill for at least 2 hours or overnight if preferred.

Set the oven temperature at moderately hot (200 C, 400 F, gas 6).

When solid, cut into 3.5-cm/1½-in squares with a wet knife (the large tin will divide into 9 squares across and 6 down). Arrange 9 gnocchi overlapping each other, in circles in oiled individual gratin dishes. Roll the trimmings into little balls with floured fingers, flatten and put one in the centre of each dish. Pour 2 tablespoons of melted butter over each gratin dish and top with grated Parmesan. The gnocchi can either be baked or frozen at this stage.

Place in the heated oven for 20 minutes or until the gnocchi are heated through and turning golden on top. If you are cooking for more than 12 and are short of oven space for the first browning, the dishes can be quickly finished off in relays under the grill. Serve each dish on an underplate.

STUFFED HAM CORNETS

ILLUSTRATED ON PAGE 36

There are a variety of fillings that can be used for these ham cornets, such as cream cheese mixed with chopped nuts and apple or celery. In the Dordogne they are often filled with pâté de foie gras. The following recipe is less luxurious but very tasty.

No. of servings	6	12	24	48
cooked ham, thinly sliced	6	12	24	48
button mushrooms	100 g/4 oz	200 g/7 oz	400 g/14 oz	800 g/1¾ lb
liver sausage	100 g/4 oz	200 g/7 oz	400 g/14 oz	800 g/1¾ lb

GARNISH *stuffed olives or gherkins; sliced cucumber, radish roses or parsley*

Trim any fat off the ham. Shape each slice into a cornet by wrapping it round a cream horn case and then removing the case.

Finely chop the mushrooms and mix them into the liver sausage. Fill the ham cornets with the mixture and place on serving plates with the join underneath. Decorate the filling at the end of the cornet with half a stuffed olive, a sliced gherkin or a slice of mushroom.

Garnish the serving plate with sliced cucumber and radish roses or parsley. Serve with crispbread or thinly sliced brown bread and butter.

—— VARIATIONS ——

Replace the liver sausage with the same quantity of curd or cream cheese. Instead of mushrooms substitute a mixture of finely chopped apples and nuts or celery heart and flavour to taste. Decorate the end of the cornets with a walnut half or dust it with paprika. Garnish the plates with tufts of fresh celery leaves.

LEEK AND CREAM TARTS

ILLUSTRATED ON PAGE 168

These creamy tarts are particularly delicious made with young leeks, but thinly sliced onion is also excellent.

No. of servings	6	12	24	48
rich shortcrust pastry	200 g/7 oz	400 g/14 oz	800 g/1¾ lb	1.6 kg/3½ lb
butter	50 g/2 oz	100 g/4 oz	200 g/7 oz	400 g/14 oz
vegetable oil	1 tablespoon	2 tablespoons	4 tablespoons	150 ml/¼ pint
leeks, white parts, finely sliced	500 g/17½ oz	1 kg/2¼ lb	2 kg/4½ lb	4 kg/9 lb
double cream	75 ml/3 fl oz	150 ml/¼ pint	300 ml/½ pint	600 ml/1 pint
single cream	75 ml/3 fl oz	150 ml/¼ pint	300 ml/½ pint	600 ml/1 pint
egg yolks	2	4	8	16
salt and pepper	to taste	to taste	to taste	to taste

GARNISH *sprinkling of nutmeg, parsley sprigs*

Make up the pastry (see page 187) and let it rest for at least an hour. Roll out very thinly and line tartlet tins measuring 20 cm (7½ ins) across the base. Ridge the edges with a fork and prick the base. Bake blind in the preheated oven, 200 C, 400 F, gas 6 for 15 minutes or until set and just colouring. Remove from the oven and lower the heat to 180 C, 350 F, gas 4.

Set the oven at moderate (180 C, 350 F, gas 4). To make the filling: heat the butter and oil in a pan, add the finely sliced leeks, cover and cook gently for 20 minutes or until softened. Stir occasionally and do not allow to brown. Mix the double and single cream together, stir in the egg yolks and gradually add this mixture to the cooked leeks. Season well with salt and freshly ground black pepper.

Remove the pastry cases from the tins and replace on a baking sheet. Carefully spoon in the filling. Return the tarts to the oven and continue baking for 20 minutes or until the filling is set and turning golden.

Garnish with a sprinkling of nutmeg and a sprig of parsley. Serve hot, allowing 1 tart per person.

NOTE: *Only ever attempt to roll out a maximum of 350 g/12 oz of pastry at a time. After cutting out 24 pastry cases, the trimmings can be kneaded together and rolled out to make more tarts.*

VARIATION

You can make an Alsatian-style tart by adding chopped lean ham to the leek filling, allowing 50 g/2 oz for every 6 tarts.

Risotto Espagnole

ILLUSTRATED ON PAGE 88

Fried savoury rice can be varied in many ways. It is an excellent way of using up stock, giblets and left-over cooked meat, or prawns. It can be made into a more satisfying dish by the addition of grated cheese and cooked smoked sausage or ham.

No. of servings	6	12	24	48
oil or butter	2 tablespoons	4 tablespoons	100 ml/3½ fl oz	200 ml/7 fl oz
onion, chopped	150 g/5 oz	300 g/11 oz	600 g/1 lb 6 oz	1.2 kg/2½ lb
rice	300 g/11 oz	600 g/1 lb 6 oz	1.2 kg/2¾ lb	2.4 kg/5½ lb
tomato juice	400 ml/14 fl oz	800 ml/1 pt 8 fl oz	1.6 litres/2¾ pints	3.2 litres/5½ pints
chicken stock, about	400 ml/14 fl oz	800 ml/1 pt 8 fl oz	1.6 litres/2¾ pints	3.2 litres/5½ pints
sliced mushrooms (optional)	100 g/4 oz	200 g/7 oz	400 g/14 oz	800 g/1¾ lb
cheese, grated	75 g/3 oz	150 g/5 oz	300 g/11 oz	600 g/1 lb 6 oz
paprika	to taste	to taste	to taste	to taste
salt and pepper	to taste	to taste	to taste	to taste

GARNISH *pepper rings*

Heat the fat and fry the onion in it until softened. Add the rice and continue frying until lightly coloured. Add the tomato juice and simmer. When the liquid has been absorbed add enough stock to cover the rice and the mushrooms if used and continue simmering and adding stock until the rice is just tender and the liquid has been absorbed. Stir in the grated cheese and cooked meats or prawns as desired. Season with paprika, salt and freshly ground black pepper. Garnish with pepper rings. Serve hot with buttered spinach or a green salad.

VARIATION

Perhaps the best known variation of this recipe is Risotto alla Milanese. This is the traditional accompaniment to Ossi bucchi (see page 89) and is excellent as a dish on its own or mixed with chicken or shellfish.

Make it as for Risotto Espagnole, but use all chicken stock and no tomato juice. When the rice is cooked, add powdered saffron to flavour and to colour the rice a soft yellow.

RICE AND CHEESE CROQUETTES

ILLUSTRATED ON PAGE 137

These savoury croquettes are called Suppli al telefono *in Italian because when they are cut open the soft Italian cheese inside has melted and stretches into strings like telephone wires. They can be made in advance and fried when required. After frying they can be frozen.*

No. of servings	6	12	24	48
Risotto Espagnole (page 23)	500 g/1 lb 2 oz	1 kg/2¼ lb	2 kg/4½ lb	4 kg/9 lb
egg, beaten	1	2	4	8
Mozarella or Bel Paese cheese, diced	250 g/9 oz	500 g/1 lb 2 oz	1 kg/2¼ lb	2 kg/4½ lb
Mortadella or any other salami or cooked ham, diced	60 g/2 oz	120 g/4 oz	250 g/9 oz	500 g/1 lb 2 oz
dried breadcrumbs	75 g/3 oz	150 g/5 oz	300 g/11 oz	600 g/1¼ lb

oil for deep frying

GARNISH *deep-fried parsley, fresh watercress or green pepper rings*

If the risotto is cold warm it and stir the egg in. Mix well and spread out to chill. Take 1 tablespoon of cold risotto and mould it in the palm of the hand. Put a cube of cheese and a cube of meat in the centre, cover with another spoonful of risotto and shape it into a ball. Continue with the rest of the risotto. You will find that 500 g/1 lb 2 oz of risotto makes 12 croquettes, allow 2 per person.

Roll the croquettes in the breadcrumbs to coat them thoroughly. At this stage the croquettes may be refrigerated, ready to fry later when they are required.

Heat the oil to moderately hot, 190 c (375 f). Arrange some croquettes in a frying basket so they are not touching. Immerse the basket carefully and completely in the fat and fry until golden brown. Drain on absorbent paper and keep warm while you fry the remainder. Serve hot garnished with parsley, watercress or green pepper rings. Accompany with green salad or buttered green beans.

HAM AND PASTA TIMBALE

ILLUSTRATED ON PAGE 45

This typically Austrian recipe can be made in individual dariole moulds and served as an hors d'oeuvre or if made in larger moulds it can be a delicious light lunch or supper dish.

No. of servings	6	12	24	48
short cut spaghetti	75 g/3 oz	150 g/5 oz	300 g/11 oz	600 g/1 lb 6 oz
oil	$\frac{1}{2}$ tablespoon	$\frac{1}{2}$ tablespoon	$\frac{1}{2}$ tablespoon	$\frac{1}{2}$ tablespoon
butter	75 g/3 oz	150 g/5 oz	300 g/11 oz	600 g/1 lb 6 oz
eggs, separated	2	4	8	16
soured cream	125 ml/4 fl oz	250 ml/8 fl oz	500 ml/17 fl oz	1 litre/1$\frac{3}{4}$ pints
cooked ham, diced	150 g/5 oz	300 g/11 oz	600 g/1 lb 6 oz	1.2 kg/2$\frac{3}{4}$ lb
parsley, chopped	2 tablespoons	4 tablespoons	25 g/1 oz	40 g/1$\frac{1}{2}$ oz
salt and pepper	to taste	to taste	to taste	to taste

dried breadcrumbs, for coating

GARNISH *fresh parsley, chopped or cress*

Set the oven at moderately hot (190 c, 375 f, gas 5).

Oil a 600-ml (1-pt) charlotte tin or individual dariole moulds (150-ml/$\frac{1}{4}$-pint size). Fill a pan with plenty of water, add salt, oil and boil. Cook the pasta in the boiling water for 10 minutes and then drain well. Cream the butter and work in the egg yolks and soured cream. Mix in the ham, pasta and parsley and season to taste with salt and freshly ground black pepper. Whisk the egg whites until stiff but not brittle and fold into the mixture.

Turn into the prepared mould and cover with breadcrumbs. Place in the heated oven and bake for 20 to 30 minutes or until set. Alternatively cook rather longer in a bain-marie. The timbale should be crisp on top but creamy inside.

Allow to shrink slightly and turn out onto a warm serving dish. Turn the small darioles out onto individual plates. Sprinkle with chopped parsley or garnish with cress.

If you are serving the timbale as a main course serve tomato sauce and buttered spinach with it. Alternatively, accompany with a tossed green salad.

ITALIAN-STYLE EGGS

This typically Italian hors d'oeuvre with its dressing of tunny fish mayonnaise is appetising and attractive. With the help of a blender mayonnaise is quickly prepared, so it is a good choice when catering for larger numbers.

No. of servings	6	12	24	48
eggs	6	12	24	48
tunny fish	75 g/3 oz	150 g/5 oz	300 g/11 oz	450 g/1 lb
mayonnaise	150 ml/$\frac{1}{4}$ pint	300 ml/$\frac{1}{2}$ pint	600 ml/1 pint	1.2 litres/2 pints
lemon juice	2 teaspoons	4 teaspoons	40 ml/1$\frac{1}{2}$ fl oz	80 ml/3 fl oz
salt and pepper	to taste	to taste	to taste	to taste
salami, sliced	40 g/1$\frac{1}{2}$ oz	75 g/3 oz	150 g/5 oz	300 g/11 oz
anchovy fillets	6	12	24	48

GARNISH *small crisp lettuce leaves or shredded lettuce*

Place the eggs in a frying basket and then into a pan with enough boiling water to cover them. Simmer very gently for 10 minutes. Remove, crack the shells and cool under running cold water. This will prevent the dark sulphur line from forming round the yolks. Shell and put in a bowl of cold water until required.

Drain the oil off the tunny fish and purée in a blender until completely smooth. Gradually stir the fish purée into the mayonnaise. Add the lemon juice and adjust the seasoning.

With a stainless steel knife dipped in cold water, cut the eggs in half lengthwise. Place two halves, cut side downwards on individual serving plates. Coat with the tuna mayonnaise. Split the anchovies and place two halves crosswise over the top of each half egg. Cut the salami slices in half, skin and arrange 6 halves round the eggs on each plate.

Garnish with small crisp lettuce leaves or shredded lettuce.

LOMBARDY TERRINE

ILLUSTRATED ON FRONT COVER AND PAGES 126–7

This terrine of veal and pork is enriched with Bel Paese cheese which comes from the Lombardy region in France.
Cook in earthenware terrines or loaf tins 21 cm × 11 cm (8½ in × 4½ in), each of which will serve 6. Leave overnight to set and mature. Serve sliced or whole, glazed and decorated and offer garlic bread or crusty rolls with it.

No. of servings	6	12	24	48
minced veal	225 g/8 oz	450 g/1 lb	900 g/2 lb	1.8 kg/4 lb
minced pork	225 g/8 oz	450 g/1 lb	900 g/2 lb	1.8 kg/4 lb
button onions or shallots, chopped	50 g/2 oz	100 g/4 oz	225 g/8 oz	450 g/1 lb
parsley, chopped	1 tablespoon	2 tablespoons	4 tablespoons	150 g/5 oz
oregano or lemon thyme	1 teaspoon	1 teaspoon	2 teaspoons	1 tablespoon
cloves garlic, crushed	1	2	4	8
salt and pepper	to taste	to taste	to taste	to taste
eggs, beaten	2	4	8	16
Bel Paese cheese, diced	100 g/4 oz	225 g/8 oz	450 g/1 lb	900 g/2 lb
cooked ham, sliced thickly, diced	2	4	8	16
button mushrooms	100 g/4 oz	225 g/8 oz	450 g/1 lb	900 g/2 lb

GARNISH *aspic jelly, ham cut into shapes, fresh herbs, lettuce leaves or curly endive*

Set the oven at moderate (180 c, 350 f, gas 4).

Mix the veal and the pork with the onions, herbs and garlic and season generously with salt and freshly ground black pepper. Add the beaten eggs and bind the mixture. Mix the cheese and the ham with the mushrooms.

Grease a terrine or loaf tin and half fill with the meat mixture. Spread the cheese filling over the minced meat and cover with the remaining meat.

Cover the terrine or loaf tin with foil and put in a bain-marie. Place in the heated oven and bake for 1½–2 hours. Leave the terrine to cool and shrink. Then remove from the container. Put the terrine into the refrigerator to mature overnight. It may be left longer if wrapped in cling film.

Garnish with ham shapes and fresh herbs, dipping each piece into liquid aspic jelly. When set, glaze completely with aspic jelly which is just about to set.

Serve the terrine whole or in slices on a narrow dish, surrounded with lettuce leaves or curly endive.

SALMON MOUSSE

ILLUSTRATED ON PAGE 17

If you are serving this mousse as a first course or for a buffet it is usually more convenient to make it in individual ramekins. As a supper dish it can be set in a mould, an aspic glaze and pattern set in the bottom and the mousse turned out upside down. If you are using canned salmon then the red kind is best.

No. of servings	6	12	24	48
fresh salmon, cooked or red canned	300 g/11 oz	600 g/1 lb 6 oz	1.2 kg/2½ lb	2.4 kg/5½ lb
liquid, fish liquor and milk	200 ml/7 fl oz	400 ml/14 fl oz	800 ml/1 pt 8 fl oz	1.6 litres/2¾ pints
butter	20 g/¾ oz	40 g/1½ oz	80 g/3 oz	160 g/5½ oz
flour	20 g/¾ oz	40 g/1½ oz	80 g/3 oz	160 g/5½ oz
boiling water	4 tablespoons	140 ml/scant ¼ pint	200 ml/7 fl oz	400 ml/14 fl oz
powdered gelatine	20 g/¾ oz	40 g/1½ oz	80 g/3 oz	160 g/5½ oz
anchovy essence	1½–2 teaspoons	3–4 teaspoons	2 tablespoons	4 tablespoons
lemon juice	to taste	to taste	to taste	to taste
salt and pepper	to taste	to taste	to taste	to taste
double cream, lightly whipped	100 ml/3½ fl oz	200 ml/7 fl oz	400 ml/14 fl oz	800 ml/1 pt 8 fl oz
egg whites	2	4	8	16
liquid aspic	200 ml/7 fl oz	400 ml/14 fl oz	800 ml/1 pt 8 fl oz	1.6 litres/2¾ pints

GARNISH *watercress leaves; cucumber crescents; tomato, sliced and deseeded or sliced lime*

If you are using canned salmon, strain off the liquid and reserve. Remove the skin and bones from the salmon and mince finely. Mix together the fish liquor and milk to make up the required quantity of liquid.

Melt the butter and blend in the flour and then the liquid, cook for 2 minutes stirring well until smooth.

Put the boiling water into a bowl and add the powdered gelatine to it and dissolve, stirring well.

Add to the sauce and stir. Mix in the salmon. Flavour to taste with anchovy essence and lemon juice and season well with salt and freshly ground pepper.

Carefully fold in the cream. Whisk the egg whites until stiff but not brittle and fold into the salmon mixture using a metal spoon.

Pour into the ramekins, smooth the top and chill until set. Meanwhile, melt the aspic jelly and cool it. If using aspic jelly crystals, follow the instructions on the packet.

Prepare the garnish design. When the mousse is set, dip each piece of garnish in liquid aspic and place it in position. Chill until set. When secure and not before, carefully spoon over a layer of cool aspic jelly and leave to set.

Serve with fleurons or thin slices of brown bread and butter.

VARIATIONS

This recipe can be adapted for smoked haddock or canned or frozen crab meat. Poach the smoked haddock and reserve the liquor. Use half fish liquor and half milk for the panada. Remember it may be salty. Prepare fish, weigh and follow above recipe.

SMOKED TROUT PÂTÉ

These little pâtés make an appetising start to a meal. With the help of a blender they can be made quickly.

No. of servings	6	12	24	48
smoked trout (about 125 g/4½ oz each)	2	4	8	16
soured cream	170 ml/6 fl oz	340 ml/12 fl oz	680 ml/1 pt 3 fl oz	1.36 litres/2½ pints
butter, softened	50 g/2 oz	100 g/4 oz	200 g/7 oz	400 g/14 oz
Fromage blanc or cottage cheese, sieved	125 g/4½ oz	250 g/9 oz	500 g/1 lb 2 oz	1 kg/2¼ lb
lemon juice	1–2 tablespoons	2–3 tablespoons	4–5 tablespoons	150 ml/¼ pint
salt and pepper	to taste	to taste	to taste	to taste

GARNISH *lemon twists and parsley spriglets*

Remove the skin and bones from the trout and put the flesh into a blender with the soured cream, butter and fromage blanc. Blend until smooth and creamy. Season to taste with lemon juice, salt and freshly ground black pepper. Fill individual ramekins with this mixture and level the top.

Garnish each pâté with a thin twist of lemon and a spriglet of parsley tucked in on each side. Serve with melba toast or thinly cut slices of hot toast made from brown bread.

VARIATION

Use smoked mackerel instead of trout. Mackerel is larger than trout, but if possible use whole fish rather than fillets.

SAVOURY CUSTARDS

In the winter, this is an excellent way of using up surplus turkey stock as it lends such a wonderful flavour to these little savoury custards. In the summer, they are delightful made with good chicken or beef stock flavoured with seasonal herbs. This Victorian recipe can also be served as a dinner savoury.

No. of servings	6	12	24	48
eggs, whole	3	6	12	24
egg yolks	4	8	16	32
good stock	900 ml/1½ pints	1.8 litres/3 pints	2.6 litres/4½ pints	5.2 litres/9¼ pints
tarragon, fresh	1 teaspoon	2 teaspoons	1 tablespoon	2 tablespoons
dried	¼ teaspoon	½ teaspoon	1 teaspoon	2 teaspoons
mint, fresh	1 teaspoon	2 teaspoons	1 tablespoon	2 tablespoons
dried	¼ teaspoon	½ teaspoon	1 teaspoon	2 teaspoons
chervil, fresh	1 teaspoon	2 teaspoons	1 tablespoon	2 tablespoon
dried	¼ teaspoon	½ teaspoon	1 teaspoon	2 teaspoons
chives, fresh	1 teaspoon	2 teaspoons	1 tablespoon	2 tablespoons
dried	¼ teaspoon	½ teaspoon	1 teaspoon	2 teaspoons
single cream	150 ml/¼ pint	300 ml/½ pint	600 ml/1 pint	1.2 litres/2 pints
salt and pepper	to taste	to taste	to taste	to taste
TOPPING				
single cream	150 ml/¼ pint	300 ml/½ pint	600 ml/1 pint	1.2 litres/2 pints
Gruyère, grated	75 g/3 oz	150 g/5 oz	300 g/11 oz	600 g/1 lb 6 oz

Set the oven at moderate (160 c, 325 f, gas 3). Beat the eggs and the yolks together lightly. Heat the stock slowly with the herbs and when boiling pour onto the eggs, beating well. Stir in the cream and adjust the seasoning. Butter 6 (125-ml/4-fl oz) sized ramekins. Pour in the mixture, straining out the herbs. The ramekins should be filled to within 1 cm/½ in of the top. Cover with a buttered paper.

Put into a bain-marie and place in the heated oven. Bake for 40 minutes or until set. Remove from the oven, coat each top with cream and sprinkle generously with grated cheese. Place in the top of a hot oven or under a grill to brown the topping. Serve with cress and cucumber sandwiches, made from thinly sliced brown bread with the crusts removed.

SOUPS

Homemade soups made from fresh ingredients are always a great success and afford plenty of scope for the creative cook. Basically, there are two categories of soup; thick ones, made from vegetable purées or a roux base, and clear ones – consommés and bouillons. The soup course leads into the meal and should whet the appetite. In a three or four course menu, allow 1.2 litres/$2\frac{1}{4}$ pints for 6 servings.

Stocks for Soups and Sauces

Many soups and sauces rely heavily on good well-flavoured stocks. These are easy to produce and you can add to them surplus tasty liquor leftover from cooking fish, meat, poultry or vegetables. Reduce this by rapid boiling and store in the freezer or for a short time in the refrigerator. Never leave stock standing about as it will collect bacteria. Cover and cool it quickly. Onion flavoured stock will ferment if not quickly stored.

The ingredients in the following recipes may be halved, but it is not usually practical to make stock in small quantities.

White Stock

White stock is used for light coloured soups and in sauces for white meats.

yields	5 litres/$8\frac{3}{4}$ pints
veal or lamb bones	1 kg/$2\frac{1}{4}$ lb
poultry carcass and giblets	
water	5 litres/$8\frac{3}{4}$ pints
carrots, peeled	150 g/5 oz
onions, peeled	150 g/5 oz
leeks (optional) trimmed, cleaned and chopped	100 g/4 oz
celery stalks, cleaned	150 g/5 oz
parsley stalks	25 g/1 oz
bouquet garni	1
black peppercorns	1 teaspoon
salt	2 teaspoons

Chop the bones, remove the fat and any marrow. This can be reserved and used for other things. Place the bones in the pan and cover with cold water. Bring to the boil and skim off the scum. Add the vegetables, whole or roughly chopped, the remaining water, the herbs and seasoning.

Cover and simmer gently for 4–6 hours. Skim again if necessary. Pour through a sieve into a cold bowl and discard the bones and vegetables.

Leave the stock to cool and the fat to rise to the surface. Meat fat will harden and should be lifted off. Poultry fat remains liquid and is removed by drawing kitchen paper across the surface of the stock until it is clear. Cover, chill rapidly and store in the refrigerator or freezer.

Brown Stock

Brown stock is a base for brown soups and sauces which accompany dark meats.

Use beef bones and the same vegetables and seasonings as for white stock.

Chop the bones, place them in a greased roasting tin and bake in the centre of a hot oven until well browned. Place in a soup pan. Brown the chopped vegetables in the fat from the bones and add to the bones. Deglaze the roasting tin with a little water and pour into the soup pan. Add the rest of the water, bring to the boil and skim. Add the herbs and seasoning and simmer for 4–6 hours.

Game Stock

Use 5 litres ($8\frac{3}{4}$ pints) of water as in the previous stock recipes. Use the carcass and giblets of game birds or trimmings and bones of hare or venison with the same vegetables and seasoning as for Brown stock and cook in the same way. Game stock should be used for game soups and sauces.

Fish Stock

Fish stock is called court bouillon in French, meaning quick broth, because it is cooked for only 20 minutes.

If fish bones are cooked for a long time the stock would become glutinous and unpalatable. Fish stock is used in making fish soups, sauces and for poaching fish.

yields	5 litres/8¾ pints
fish bones, heads or trimmings	2 kg/4½ lb
water	5 litres/8¾ pints
onion, peeled	150 g/5 oz
celery stalks, cleaned	2
parsley stalks	25 g/1 oz
bay leaf	1
white peppercorns	12
salt	4 teaspoons
white wine or	50 ml/8 fl oz
white wine vinegar	2 tablespoons
sliced, unpeeled lemon	½

Place all the ingredients in a soup pan. Bring to the boil, skim and simmer, uncovered, for 20 minutes. Strain and use as required. Once the bones are removed the stock can be reduced for sauces or for storing.

Shell Fish Stock for Bisque

Use the shells of lobster, crab or crayfish instead of white fish bones. If you don't have enough shell fish shells you can use a small proportion of white fish bones to make up the weight.

Shell fish stock is made in the same way as fish stock but it is cooked for 1 hour before being strained.

SPICED LENTIL SOUP

This is a satisfying soup which can also be made with vegetable stock instead of ham or duck.

No. of servings	6	12	24	48
cooking apples	450 g/1 lb	900 g/2 lb	1.5 kg/3 lb	2.1 kg/4½ lb
bacon dripping or butter	50 g/2 oz	100 g/4 oz	175 g/6 oz	350 g/12 oz
celery, chopped	100 g/4 oz	200 g/7 oz	350 g/12 oz	700 g/1½ lb
onion, chopped	300 g/11 oz	600 g/1 lb 6 oz	1.5 kg/2¼ lb	2.1 kg/4½ lb
carrots, chopped	50 g/2 oz	75 g/3 oz	100 g/4 oz	175 g/6 oz
orange lentils, washed and drained	225 g/8 oz	450 g/1 lb	800 g/1¾ lb	1.6 kg/3½ lb
curry powder, mild	2 teaspoons	4 teaspoons	1½ tablespoons	3 tablespoons
ham or duck stock	1.5 litres/2¾ pints	3 litres/5¼ pints	4.5 litres/8 pints	9 litres/16 pints
salt	2 teaspoons	1 tablespoon	35 g/1 oz	70 g/2½ oz
ground black pepper	¼ teaspoon	½ teaspoon	1 teaspoon	1½ teaspoons

GARNISH *chopped crisp streaky bacon rashers or croûtons fried in garlic butter*

Peel, core and roughly chop the apples. Heat the fat and fry the celery, onion and carrots gently until the onion is softened, but not coloured. Add the apples and stir until well coated with fat. Mix in the lentils and curry powder and continue cooking over a moderate heat for 5 minutes. Add the stock and bring it slowly to the boil, cover and simmer gently for 1–1½ hours. Liquidise the soup or pass it through a mouli-légumes. Season and reheat.

Serve the soup in bowls garnished with crispy bacon or croûtons.

Russian Fish Pie (see page 68) and Winter Salad (see page 143)

Savoury Samosas (see page 150); Stuffed Eggs (see page 154); Mushroom Puffs (see page 157) and Stuffed Ham Cornets (see page 21)

CREAM OF VEGETABLE SOUP

ILLUSTRATED ON PAGE 156

This is a very versatile vegetable soup recipe which can be adapted to whatever vegetables are in season. In summer it is delicious made with fresh herbs using twice the quantity given for dried.

No. of servings	6	12	24	48
pork or beef dripping or margarine	40 g/1½ oz	80 g/3 oz	150 g/5 oz	280 g/10 oz
onions, chopped	200 g/7 oz	400 g/14 oz	700 g/1½ lb	1.4 kg/3 lb
leeks, chopped	200 g/7 oz	400 g/14 oz	700 g/1½ lb	1.4 kg/3 lb
celery, chopped	200 g/7 oz	400 g/14 oz	700 g/1½ lb	1.4 kg/3 lb
potatoes, chopped	200 g/7 oz	400 g/14 oz	700 g/1½ lb	1.4 kg/3 lb
mixture of carrots, turnips, parsnips or swedes, chopped	250 g/9 oz	500 g/1 lb 12 oz	875 g/1 lb 15 oz	1.75 kg/2¾ lb
mixed herbs	1 teaspoon	2 teaspoons	3 teaspoons	6 teaspoons
white stock or half quantity of canned tomatoes and half of water	1 litre/1¾ pints	2 litres/3½ pints	3.5 litres/6 pints	7 litres/12 pints
parsley, chopped	20 g/¾ oz	40 g/1½ oz	70 g/2½ oz	140 g/5 oz
salt and pepper	to taste	to taste	to taste	to taste
single cream	100 ml/3½ fl oz	200 ml/7 fl oz	350 ml/12 fl oz	700 ml/1¼ pints

GARNISH *croûtons and chopped chives*

Heat the fat in a soup pan and cook the onions, leeks and celery gently in it until slightly softened but not coloured. Stir in the potatoes, root vegetables and mixed herbs and cook for 5 minutes, stirring frequently. Add the stock or tomato juice and water, bring to the boil and add the parsley. Cover and simmer for about 45 minutes or until all the vegetables are cooked.

Liquidise the soup and return it to the pan. Thin as required and adjust the seasoning, add the cream, bring to the simmer but do not allow to boil. Serve with croûtons.

CONSOMMÉ MADRILÈNE

Consommés are refined soups made from a good basic beef or chicken stock. Each one gets its own particular name from the garnish used. A dish which is à la Madrilène always contains tomatoes. This soup is often served en tasse, in small cups, either hot or lightly jellied if cold.

No. of servings	6	12	24	48
egg whites	2	4	6	12
water	.5 litre/17 fl oz	1 litre/1¾ pints	1.5 litres/2¼ pints	3 litres/5 pints
shin of beef, minced	225 g/8 oz	450 g/1 lb	675 g/1½ lb	1.3 kg/2¾ lb
salt	1 teaspoon	2 teaspoons	3 teaspoons	5 teaspoons
onion, skinned	100 g/4 oz	200 g/7 oz	350 g/12 oz	700 g/1½ lb
carrots, chopped	100 g/4 oz	200 g/7 oz	350 g/12 oz	700 g/1½ lb
celery, chopped	200 g/7 oz	450 g/1 lb	675 g/1½ lb	1.3 kg/2¾ lb
pimento, chopped	50 g/2 oz	100 g/4 oz	175 g/6 oz	350 g/12 oz
tomatoes	200 g/7 oz	450 g/1 lb	675 g/1½ lb	1.3 kg/2¾ lb
chicken stock	1 litre/1¾ pints	2 litres/3½ pints	3 litres/5¼ pints	6 litres/10½ pints
bouquet garni	1	1	2	2
black peppercorns	5	10	15	30
powdered gelatine (if serving cold)	1 teaspoon	2 teaspoons	30 g/1 oz	40 g/1½ oz

GARNISH *juliennes of celery; skinned seedless tomatoes; finely shredded sorrel or soup pasta*

Place the egg whites in the soup pan with the water and whisk well. Add the beef and salt and mix thoroughly, breaking down the mince. Grease a pan and heat it. Halve the onion and brown it in the pan. Add this to the soup along with the carrot, celery and pimento. Peel and chop the tomatoes and add them with the stock and bouquet garni. Bring the soup to the boil, stirring carefully. Immediately it comes to the boil, remove the spatula and leave the scum to rise and coagulate. Simmer very gently for 1½–2 hours. Place a double muslin in a sieve or colander and carefully strain off the consommé without breaking the crust or the consommé will be cloudy. Remove the fat by passing kitchen paper across the consommé. Adjust the seasoning and add sherry if used.

If you are serving this soup hot, cook the juliennes of celery and then add them to the consommé along with the skinned tomatoes cut into strips.

If it is to be served cold, dissolve the gelatine thoroughly in a little of the hot soup and stir it into the consommé, mixing well. Pour into soup bowls and chill thoroughly. When serving, garnish with a teaspoon of soured cream, topped with chopped chives or mock caviar (lump fish roe).

Danish Blue Cheese and Cauliflower Soup

This is a more exciting version of cauliflower soup than the classic French crème Dubarry. Toasted flaked almonds make an admirable crispy contrast to the creamy soup and are a change from croûtons.

No. of servings	6	12	24	48
medium cauliflower	1	2	4	7
chicken stock	1.5 litres/2¾ pints	3 litres/5 pints	5.25 litres/9 pints 3 fl oz	10.5 litres/18 pints 6 fl oz
butter	50 g/2 oz	100 g/4 oz	175 g/6 oz	350 g/12 oz
onion, chopped	100 g/4 oz	200 g/7 oz	350 g/12 oz	700 g/1½ lb
flour	50 g/2 oz	100 g/4 oz	175 g/6 oz	350 g/12 oz
Danish Blue, grated	50 g/2 oz	100 g/4 oz	175 g/6 oz	350 g/12 oz
pepper (optional)	to taste	to taste	to taste	to taste

GARNISH *flaked almonds, toasted*

Trim off the coarse outer leaves and divide the cauliflower into florets and wash thoroughly. Heat up the stock and put in the cauliflower, cover and simmer gently for 10–15 minutes until just tender. Purée in a liquidiser. Melt the butter in the soup pan and fry the onion gently until softened, but do not allow it to colour. Gradually blend in the flour and when smooth, cook, stirring for 3 minutes.

Gradually mix in the cauliflower purée and cook gently for another 3 minutes. Add the grated cheese bit by bit and stir until dissolved.

Adjust the seasoning. As the cheese is salty no additional salt is usually needed, but you may want to add some freshly ground black pepper.

Warm soup bowls. Toast the flaked almonds under the grill or in a hot oven. Pour the soup into the bowls and garnish with the toasted almonds.

CHESTNUT AND APPLE SOUP

Turkey stock (see page 32) is particularly good in this delicious winter soup.

No. of servings	6	12	24	48
chestnuts, shelled	450 g/1 lb	1 kg/2¼ lb	1.75 kg/3¾ lb	3.5 kg/8 lb
turkey or ham stock	1.2 litres/2¼ pints	2.4 litres/4½ pints	4.2 litres/7¼ pints	8.4 litres/1 gallon 6½ pints
dried mixed herbs	1 teaspoon	2 teaspoons	3–4 teaspoons	3–4 tablespoons
turkey fat or margarine	50 g/2 oz	100 g/4 oz	175 g/6 oz	350 g/12 oz
celery, chopped	150 g/5 oz	300 g/11 oz	525 g/18 oz	1 kg/2¼ lb
onion, chopped	75 g/3 oz	150 g/5 oz	360 g/12 oz	500 g/18 oz
cooking apples, sliced	450 g/1 lb	1 kg/2¼ lb	1.75 kg/3¾ lb	3.5 kg/8 lb
lemon juice	2 tablespoons	4 tablespoons	100 ml/3½ fl oz	200 ml/7 fl oz
salt and freshly ground black pepper	to taste	to taste	to taste	to taste
single cream	100 ml/3½ fl oz	200 ml/7 fl oz	350 ml/12 fl oz	700 ml/1¼ pints

GARNISH *fried croûtons, chipolatas*

Boil the chestnuts in the stock with the herbs for 1 hour until tender.

Heat the fat and cook the celery, apples and onion in it until softened. Add this to the soup and continue cooking for 20 minutes. Liquidise.

Return the soup to the pan, sharpen to taste with lemon juice and correct the seasoning. Mix a little soup into the cream and stir into the rest of the soup. Heat through without boiling and garnish with fried croûtons or fried chopped chipolatas.

NOTE: *To skin the chestnuts cut a cross in the top of each chestnut and roast it in a hot oven (220 C, 425 F, gas 7) for 15–20 minutes until they split. Alternatively, you can fry them in a little fat.*

Dried chestnuts can be used quite successfully for savoury purées, especially when they are cooked in stock. Unsweetened canned chestnuts are not so tasty and as they have already been pressure cooked, they cannot be simmered for long.

CURRIED APPLE SOUP

ILLUSTRATED ON PAGE 76

This is a splendid spicy winter soup. Vegetarians can use a vegetable stock instead of a meat one and could substitute croûtons fried in garlic butter for the crisp bacon garnish.

No. of servings	6	12	24	48
cooking apples	450 g/1 lb	900 g/2 lb	1.5 kg/3 lb	2.7 kg/6 lb
bacon dripping or butter	50 g/2 oz	100 g/4 oz	175 g/6 oz	350 g/12 oz
chopped celery	100 g/4 oz	225 g/8 oz	350 g/12 oz	675 g/1½ lb
chopped carrots	50 g/2 oz	75 g/3 oz	100 g/4 oz	175 g/6 oz
chopped onion	225 g/8 oz	350 g/12 oz	450 g/1 lb	675 g/1½ lb
orange lentils, washed and drained	225 g/8 oz	350 g/12 oz	560 g/1¼ lb	1 kg/2¼ lb
curry powder	2 teaspoons	1 tablespoon	1½ tablespoons	3 tablespoons
ham or duck stock	1.5 litres/2¾ pints	3 litres/5 pints	4.5 litres/8 pints	9 litres/16 pints
salt and freshly ground pepper	to taste	to taste	to taste	to taste
GARNISH				
streaky bacon rashers	6	12	24	48

Peel, core and roughly chop the apples. Heat the fat in a large thick pan and fry the celery, carrots and onion until softened. Add the apples and stir until well covered with fat. Mix in the lentils and curry powder and continue cooking over a moderate heat for 5 minutes. Add the stock and seasoning. Bring slowly to the boil, cover and simmer gently for 1–1½ hours. Liquidise and if desired sieve and return to the pan. Adjust the seasoning and the consistency and reheat.

Grill or fry the streaky bacon until very crisp. Chop and sprinkle on the soup as a garnish.

FREEZING NOTE: *When cooked, cool the soup rapidly and pour into containers, allowing enough room for it to expand during freezing. Freeze the garnish in separate containers. When reheating adjust the seasoning and if necessary add extra stock. Reheat the bacon garnish in a hot oven (230C, 450F, gas 8) for 10 minutes.*

Summer Borshch

There are many variations of this Russian beetroot soup. There is a Polish version of it which starts off with a whole duck of which the flesh is finely shredded and added to the soup. The following recipe is not so robust, but a good duck stock certainly makes an excellent base. Alternatively, use a strong beef or chicken stock. This version can be served hot or cold.

No. of servings	**6**	**12**	**24**	**48**
raw beetroot	500 g/18 oz	1 kg/2¼ lb	1.75 kg/3¾ lb	3.5 kg/7¾ lb
duck, beef or chicken stock	1.5 litres/2¾ pints	3 litres/5¼ pints	5.5 litres/9½ pints	11 litres/19¼ pints
onion, finely chopped	150 g/5 oz	300 g/11 oz	525 g/18½ oz	1 kg/2¼ lb
leek, finely chopped	50 g/2 oz	100 g/4 oz	175 g/6 oz	350 g/12 oz
celery, finely chopped	50 g/2 oz	100 g/4 oz	175 g/6 oz	350 g/12 oz
carrots, thinly sliced	50 g/2 oz	100 g/4 oz	175 g/6 oz	350 g/12 oz
potatoes, diced	50 g/2 oz	100 g/4 oz	175 g/6 oz	350 g/12 oz
bay leaf	1	2	2	2
tomato purée	4 teaspoons	2½ tablespoons	4½ tablespoons	140 ml/4½ fl oz
caster sugar	1 teaspoon	2 teaspoons	3 teaspoons	4 teaspoons
lemon juice	1 tablespoon	2 tablespoons	4 tablespoons	8 tablespoons
soured cream	150 ml/¼ pint	300 ml/½ pint	400 ml/14 fl oz	800 ml/1½ pints
parsley, chopped	1 tablespoon	2 tablespoons	3½ tablespoons	7 tablespoons
salt and pepper	to taste	to taste	to taste	to taste

GARNISH *for hot soup: chopped fresh mint or chives. For cold soup: a little extra soured cream, sieved hard-boiled egg yolk and chopped chives*

Peel the beetroot, reserve a fifth of it and dice the remainder. Put the stock in a soup pan and add the prepared vegetables and herbs, cover and simmer for 30 minutes. Mix together the tomato purée, sugar and lemon juice, add a little soup and stir the mixture into the soup. Bring to the simmer, season to taste, and continue cooking gently until the vegetables are tender.

Ten minutes before serving, grate the remaining beetroot into the soup and continue cooking, this will improve the colour.

Stir a little soup into the soured cream and blend this mixture into the soup. Adjust the seasoning and the consistency, adding a little more stock if required. Heat through but do not boil.

If serving cold, top with a swirl of extra soured cream and garnish with a sieved hard-boiled yolk and chives.

FRENCH ONION SOUP

This tasty warming soup was a well known favourite with the porters at Les Halles, the famous vegetable market in Paris. It would sustain them on cold winter mornings and also became fashionable with late revellers on the way home. It was adopted by the English and became the smart way to round off all-night dancing at society balls. It is also ideal for Guy Fawkes parties.

No. of servings	6	12	24	48
Spanish onions	500 g/18 oz	1 kg/2¼ lb	1.75 kg/4 lb	3.5 kg/8 lb
lard	50 g/2 oz	100 g/4 oz	175 g/6 oz	350 g/12 oz
brown stock	1.5 litres/2¼ pints	3 litres/5¼ pints	5.25 litres/7 pints	10.5 litres/18 pints 14 fl oz
salt and freshly ground black pepper	to taste	to taste	to taste	to taste
CROÛTES DE FLÛTES				
thin slices of flûte	12	24	48	96
Gruyère or Parmesan, grated	40 g/1½ oz	80 g/3 oz	140 g/5 oz	240 g/9 oz

Peel and thinly slice the onions. Heat the lard and add the onions. Stir over a gentle heat until golden. Heat the stock and add it, cover and simmer gently until the onions are softened, 20–30 minutes. Set the oven at hot (220 C, 425 F, gas 7). Remove any surplus fat with kitchen paper and season. Slice the *flûte* (this is a thin French loaf) diagonally and sprinkle generously with grated cheese. Bake the croûtes in the heated oven until golden brown. Warm marmites or soup bowls and ladle the soup into them. Place two croûtes on each one.

NOTE: *If you want strings in the soup, put an extra spoonful of cheese in the bottom of each bowl before ladling in the soup.*

SCALLOP AND ARTICHOKE SOUP

ILLUSTRATED ON PAGE 138

This is a delicious lunch or dinner party soup. Toasted flaked almonds make a more attractive garnish than the ubiquitous chopped parsley.

No. of servings	6	12	24	48
butter	75 g/3 oz	175 g/6 oz	275 g/10 oz	550 g/1 lb 3 oz
onion, chopped	100 g/4 oz	225 g/8 oz	350 g/12 oz	575 g/1¼ lb
Jerusalem artichokes	500 g/1 lb 2 oz	1 kg/2¼ lb	1.8 kg/4 lb	3.6 kg/8 lb
potatoes	225 g/8 oz	450 g/1 lb	1.35 kg/3 lb	2.7 kg/6 lb
fish or chicken stock	900 ml/1½ pints	1.75 litres/3 pints	2.75 litres/4½ pints	5.5 litres/9 pints 7 fl oz
scallops	5	10	15	30
milk	225 ml/8 fl oz	500 ml/16 fl oz	700 ml/1 pint 4 fl oz	1.5 litres/2½ pints
egg yolks	2	4	6	12
double cream	150 ml/¼ pint	300 ml/½ pint	450 ml/¾ pint	900 ml/1½ pints
salt and pepper	to taste	to taste	to taste	to taste

GARNISH *chopped parsley and scallop coral*

Melt the butter and cook the onion in it until transparent. Add the peeled and sliced Jerusalem artichokes and potato. Cook, stirring, until well buttered. Cover and cook gently for 15 minutes. Add the stock, cover and continue cooking for 20 minutes or until softened. Liquidise and sieve if desired. Return to the pan and season to taste.

Set the scallop corals aside. Poach the white part of the scallops lightly in the milk. Dice and add them with the milk to the soup and heat gently. Beat the egg yolks into the cream, stir into the soup and cook gently until the soup thickens. Do not boil it or the soup may curdle. Adjust the seasoning and just before serving add the uncooked scallop corals. If they are too large cut them up.

Garnish with chopped parsley and scallop coral.

ABOVE: *Iced Mushroom Soup (see page 51); Ham and Pasta Timbale (see page 25)*
OVERLEAF: *Florida Fruit Cocktail (see page 14); Greek Rice Salad (see page 142); Chaudfroid of Salmon Trout (see page 67) and Gâteau St Honoré (see page 160)*

Chicken with Lemon Sauce (see page 109); Glazed Carrots (see page 132); Casseroled Courgettes (see page 133) and Apricot Charlotte Russe (see page 169)

BISQUE OF SHELLFISH

ILLUSTRATED ON PAGE 125

Bisque is a rich soup made from fish. It is particularly good when made with shellfish, lobster, crayfish or crab.

No. of servings	6	12	24	48
lobster or crayfish	500 g/17½ oz	1 kg/2¼ lb	1.75 kg/3¾ lb	3.5 kg/8 lb
button mushrooms	50 g/2 oz	100 g/4 oz	175 g/6 oz	350 g/12 oz
butter	50 g/2 oz	100 g/4 oz	175 g/6 oz	350 g/12 oz
celery, finely chopped	50 g/2 oz	100 g/4 oz	175 g/6 oz	350 g/12 oz
carrots, finely chopped	50 g/2 oz	100 g/4 oz	175 g/6 oz	350 g/12 oz
onion, chopped	100 g/4 oz	200 g/7 oz	350 g/12 oz	700 g/1½ lb
brandy	50 ml/2 fl oz	50 ml/2 fl oz	75 ml/3 fl oz	150 ml/¼ pint
dry white wine	150 ml/¼ pint	300 ml/½ pint	525 ml/1 pint	1.5 litres/2½ pints
tomatoes, canned	400 g/14 oz	800 g/1¾ lb	1.3 kg/3 lb	2.6 kg/6 lb
fish stock	1.2 litres/1 quart	2.4 litres/2 quarts	4.2 litres/3½ quarts	8.4 litres/7 quarts
thyme, dried	½ teaspoon	1 teaspoon	1½ teaspoons	3 teaspoons
basil, dried	½ teaspoon	1 teaspoon	1½ teaspoons	3 teaspoons
salt and pepper	to taste	to taste	to taste	to taste
ground rice	80 g/3 oz	160 g/6 oz	280 g/10 oz	560 g/1¼ lb
double cream	75 ml/3 fl oz	150 ml/6 fl oz	275 ml/9 fl oz	550 ml/18 fl oz
lemon juice	to taste	to taste	to taste	to taste

GARNISH *chopped fresh parsley and grated lemon rind*

Clean fish, leaving in their shells. Remove the sack from lobster. Remove intestine and chop tail.

Chop mushrooms. Melt butter, fry mushrooms with celery, carrots and onion until golden, add fish, fry 10 minutes. Warm brandy, pour over and ignite. When flames die, add wine, tomatoes, stock, herbs and seasoning. Bring to the boil, simmer for 20 minutes.

Lift out fish. Separate the meat from the shells.

Chop the meat, crush shells thoroughly. Return both to the pan, simmer for a further 10–25 minutes. Purée in a liquidiser or a mouli-légumes, return to the pan. Mix the ground rice to a smooth paste with a little of the soup and stir back into the pan. Simmer 5 minutes.

Stir cream into the pan, heat through, but do not boil. Sharpen with lemon juice. Garnish with fresh parsley and grated lemon rind.

CUCUMBER AND GREEN PEA SOUP

ILLUSTRATED ON PAGES 166–7

This fresh green soup is best served cold, but may be heated if desired. In summer the chilled soup looks particularly attractive if each bowl is served in a bed of cracked ice garnished with fresh mint leaves.

No. of servings	6	12	24	48
butter or margarine	50 g/2 oz	100 g/4 oz	175 g/6 oz	350 g/12 oz
onion, chopped	100 g/4 oz	200 g/8 oz	350 g/12 oz	700 g/1½ lb
streaky bacon rashers or ham trimmings	2	4	8	12
lettuce, shredded	1 small	1 large	2 medium	3 large
canned peas, reserve liquid	400 g/14 oz	800 g/1¾ lb	1.2 kg/2¾ lb	2.4 kg/5¼ lb
flour, about	25 g/1 oz	50 g/2 oz	75 g/3 oz	150 g/5 oz
milk	300 ml/½ pint	600 ml/1 pint	1 litre/1¾ pints	2.1 litres/3½ pints
white stock, about	300 ml/½ pint	600 ml/1 pint	1 litre/1¾ pints	2.1 litres/3½ pints
cucumber	1	2	3½	7
mint, chopped fresh	1 tablespoon	2 tablespoons	3½ tablespoons	7 tablespoons
dried	1 teaspoon	2 teaspoons	3½ teaspoons	7 teaspoons
salt	to taste	to taste	to taste	to taste
lemon juice	to taste	to taste	to taste	to taste

GARNISH *soured cream and cucumber, slices of paprika or fresh mint*

Heat the fat in a soup pan and cook the onion and bacon slowly in it until the fat runs from the bacon. Do not allow it to brown or the soup will lose its fresh green colour. Add the lettuce, cover and sweat over a low heat until bright green.

Remove the pan from the heat. Stir in the drained, canned peas and enough flour to absorb the fat. Blend in the milk, bring to the boil, stirring steadily then add the pea liquid and thin as required with stock. Grate half the cucumber, unpeeled, into the soup. Add the mint and season to taste. Cover and simmer gently for 30 minutes. If it is boiled too rapidly the soup will separate.

Pass the soup through a mouli-légumes or liquidise. Peel, grate and add the remaining cucumber. Sharpen to taste with lemon juice and chill thoroughly. Taste before serving as chilling tends to reduce the flavour.

Pour into chilled soup cups. Add a swirl of cream and top with a thin slice of cucumber or sprinkle with chopped fresh mint or paprika. For special occasions place each soup cup in a larger dish or bowl and surround with cracked ice garnished with fresh mint leaves.

ICED MUSHROOM SOUP

ILLUSTRATED ON PAGE 45

In this recipe the mushroom purée is barely cooked and this gives the soup its deliciously fresh taste. It is important to use a strong well-flavoured chicken stock. If fresh tarragon is not available then frozen tarragon is preferable to dried.

No. of servings	6	12	24	48
butter	40 g/1½ oz	75 g/3 oz	125 g/4½ oz	250 g/9 oz
flour	40 g/1½ oz	75 g/3 oz	125 g/4½ oz	250 g/9 oz
chicken stock	1 litre/1¾ pints	2 litres/3½ pints	3 litres/5¼ pints	6 litres/10½ pints
tarragon, chopped, fresh or frozen	1½ tablespoons	3 tablespoons	5 tablespoons	10 tablespoons
white mushrooms	250 g/9 oz	500 g/18 oz	800 g/1¾ lb	1.75 kg/3½ lb
single cream	300 ml/½ pint	600 ml/1 pint	850 ml/1½ pints	1.7 litres/3 pints
salt and pepper	to taste	to taste	to taste	to taste

GARNISH *cream and toasted flaked almonds*

Make a smooth white roux with the butter and flour. Then blend in the chicken stock and add the chopped tarragon. Bring to the boil, stirring steadily. Simmer gently for 15–20 minutes, stirring occasionally. Wash the mushrooms and purée them in a blender or mouli-légumes. Add them to the soup with the cream and simmer gently for 5 minutes. Check the consistency. Chill thoroughly, adjust the seasoning. Serve in consommé cups and garnish with a swirl of cream and toasted flaked almonds

Gazpacho Andaluz

ILLUSTRATED ON PAGE 57

There are various versions of this Spanish salad soup. Well chilled it is excellent in hot weather. The garnishes are served separately in little bowls for the guests to help themselves. It is particularly good for outdoor meals and barbecues.

No. of servings	6	12	24	48
tomatoes, fresh or canned	450 g/1 lb	1 kg/2 lb	1.75 kg/3½ lb	3.5 kg/7 lb
cucumber	1	2	3	6
onion, large	½	1	2	3
green or red pepper	2	4	6	12
brown bread, slices	2	4	6	12
garlic cloves	1	2	3	6
wine vinegar	2 tablespoons	4 tablespoons	90 ml/3¼ fl oz	180 ml/6 fl oz
olive oil	50 ml/2 fl oz	100 ml/3½ fl oz	150 ml/¼ pint	300 ml/½ pint
salt and freshly ground black pepper	to taste	to taste	to taste	to taste
chicken stock, as required				
ice cubes	225 g/½ lb	450 g/1 lb	675 g/1½ lb	1.5 kg/3 lb

GARNISH *chopped peppers; spring onions, chopped; toasted croûtons*

Peel and chop the tomatoes, cucumber and onion. Scald, peel, seed and chop the peppers. Remove the crusts from the bread and pull into pieces. Put all the ingredients into a liquidiser and blend into a smooth purée, adding stock as necessary. For large quantities purée in batches. Chill thoroughly and adjust the seasoning. Just before serving, add ice cubes.

Accompany with little bowls of chopped peppers, spring onions (including the green part), and toasted croûtons.

NOTE: *If you are using canned tomatoes use them with their juice. They are preferable to under-ripe fresh tomatoes, giving a better colour and flavour.*

FISH

There are a huge variety of fish and shellfish
which can be prepared as an hors d'oeuvre or as
a main course. For filleted fish allow
90–100 g/3–4 oz per portion. For cuts on the
bone, 150–200 g/6–8 oz per portion. For whole
fish, such as mackerel and trout allow
200–250 g/8–10 oz per portion. To judge whether
a fish is fresh check that it has a fresh smell, clear
eyes, red gills, shining scales and firm flesh.

SCALLOPS COQUILLES ST JACQUES

ILLUSTRATED ON PAGE 116

When buying fresh scallops allow 1½–2 per person. Ask the fishmonger to give you the deep shells for serving. Afterwards keep and clean these for occasions when you have to rely on frozen scallops which are sold without shells.
Scallops make an elegant dinner party hors d'oeuvre. If you are going to serve potatoes with the main course, you could garnish the scallops with garden cress instead of Duchess potatoes.

No. of servings	6	12	24	48
scallops, shelled	350 g/12 oz	700 g/1½ lb	1.4 kg/3 lb	2.8 kg/6 lb
dry white wine	150 ml/¼ pint	300 ml/½ pint	600 ml/1 pint	1.2 litres/2 pints
shallots or small onions	1	2	4	8
parsley stalks	3	6	15 g/½ oz	30 g/1 oz
bay leaf	1	2	3	4
sliver of lemon rind	1	2	3	4
salt and peppercorns	to taste	to taste	to taste	to taste
SAUCE				
mushrooms	175 g/6 oz	350 g/12 oz	700 g/1½ lb	1.4 kg/3 lb
butter	50 g/2 oz	100 g/4 oz	200 g/7 oz	400 g/14 oz
onion, finely chopped	1 tablespoon	2 tablespoons	4 tablespoons	100 g/4 oz
plain flour	50 g/2 oz	100 g/4 oz	200 g/7 oz	400 g/14 oz
milk	200 ml/7 fl oz	400 ml/14 fl oz	800 ml/1 pint 8 fl oz	1.6 litres/2¾ pints
scallop liquor, about	450 ml/¾ pint	900 ml/1½ pints	1.8 litres/3 pints	3.5 litres/6 pints
lemon juice	to taste	to taste	to taste	to taste
salt and pepper	to taste	to taste	to taste	to taste
dried breadcrumbs	30 g/1½ oz	60 g/2½ oz	120 g/4½ oz	240 g/8½ oz

DUCHESS POTATOES

mashed potatoes	450 g/1 lb	900 g/2 lb	1.8 kg/4 lb	3.6 kg/8 lb
butter	40 g/1½ oz	80 g/3 oz	160 g/5½ oz	300 g/11 oz
egg yolk	1	2	4	8
milk, about	30 ml/1½ fl oz	60 ml/3 fl oz	120 ml/4 fl oz	240 ml/7 fl oz
salt and black pepper	to taste	to taste	to taste	to taste

GARNISH *scallop coral; toasted crumbs*

Remove the gills on the scallops and the black muscle and rinse them in cold water. Place them in a saucepan with the wine, shallots, herbs, lemon rind and enough water to cover them. Season. Cover and poach gently for 12 minutes or until just tender. Strain and reserve the cooking liquid.

To make the sauce: wash the mushrooms, and slice thinly. Melt the butter, fry the mushrooms and onions in it until softened. Draw the pan from the heat and add the flour and blend into a smooth roux. Gradually stir in the milk and cook until thickened. Bit by bit, add enough scallop liquid to make a coating sauce. Sharpen with lemon juice and adjust the seasoning.

To dress: put a large spoonful of sauce in each clean shell. Slice the scallops thickly and divide between the shells, reserving one orange coral as a garnish for each one. Cover with sauce, leaving a margin round the edge for a potato or cress border. Cover straightaway with toasted crumbs before a skin forms.

Make up the Duchess potatoes by adding the butter, egg yolks and milk to the mashed potatoes until you get a piping consistency. Season well. Pipe round the edge of the shell, except the top. Place spare coral at the top of the shell. The scallop can be frozen at this point.

When serving, heat the scallops through in a hot oven until the potato is golden, or finish browning under the grill.

Garnish with scallop coral.

—————— VARIATIONS ——————

Instead of scallops you can use scampi or white crab meat. To make seafood scallops use a mixture of scallops, scampi and prawns. You can also fill scallop shells with poached firm white fish, turbot, halibut, hake or large cod. Make a mushroom sauce with half fish stock and half milk and dress on the shell as you would scallops.

DRESSED CRAB

ILLUSTRATED ON PAGE 168

If you are serving dressed crab as a main course for a lunch or buffet supper, buy small crabs weighing about 575 g/1¼ lb each so that they can be served in their shell. For a first course larger crabs may be more economical and can be picked and divided into scallop shells, allowing about 100 g/4 oz of crab meat per person.

No. of servings	6	12	24	48
crab, boiled (about 575 g/1¼ lb each)	6	12	24	48
lemon juice	90 ml/3 fl oz	180 ml/6 fl oz	300 ml/½ pint	600 ml/1 pint
salad oil	180 ml/6 fl oz	350 ml/12 fl oz	600 ml/1 pint	1.2 litres/2 pints
fresh brown breadcrumbs	75 g/3 oz	175 g/6 oz	350 g/12 oz	725 g/1½ lb
salt and black pepper	to taste	to taste	to taste	to taste
lemon juice	to taste	to taste	to taste	to taste

GARNISH *paprika; hard-boiled eggs; chopped parsley; lemon wedges; watercress or lettuce leaves*

To pick out the crab meat first wash the cooked crab and then place it shell side down on a board. Twist off the legs and both claws. Reserve the legs for decoration. Crack the claws with a claw cracker or a hammer and extract the meat. Carefully scrape out of crevices using a lobster pick or a steel skewer or a teaspoon handle.

Holding the crab shell side down with your fingers, use your thumbs to push the centre body up and out from the side opposite the eyes. Discard the stomach sack which lies behind the head and the gills, the so-called dead man's fingers, which lie along both sides of the undercarriage. With a spoon scrape out the brown meat from the shell and keep this separate from the white meat. Pick out the white meat left in the leg sockets. With a small hammer or knife handle tap round the natural line of the undershell. Wash the shell thoroughly and polish it with a little oil rubbed in with kitchen paper.

Make a dressing with the oil and lemon juice to use for dressing the crab. Shred the white meat with two forks and season it with the dressing. Mix the brown meat with the brown bread-crumbs, salt, black pepper and add lemon juice to taste.

Place the brown meat down the centre of the shell and arrange the white meat on either side. Garnish the centre with criss-cross lines of paprika. Sieve the egg yolks and chop the whites. Between the brown and the white meats, arrange on either side a border of sieved yolk, then a line of chopped whites and finally a band of chopped parsley.

Serve garnished with the crab legs, lemon wedges and watercress or lettuce leaves. Serve with brown bread and butter.

Gazpacho Andaluz (see page 52)

Toulouse-style Cassoulet (see page 78); Pears Baked in
Cider (see page 175) and Lemon Flummery (see page 173)

SOLE VÉRONIQUE

This dish can be served either as a first course or as the fish course in a formal lunch or dinner. In either case serve half the quantity of fish given below. It also makes a good light main course at lunch. The delicate white wine sauce is thickened with egg yolks and cream, not flour, so it will not freeze. If you plan to reheat it, use a bain-marie as direct heat will curdle it.

Buy sole on the bone, each one weighing about 650 g/1½ lb. Get them filleted into four fillets, each of these should weigh about 100 g/4 oz. Keep the skin and bones for making the court bouillon.

No. of servings	6	12	24	48
court bouillon (page 33)				
sole (about 650 g/1½ lb each)	3	6	12	24
lemons	1	2	3	6
salt and black pepper	to taste	to taste	to taste	to taste
butter	25 g/1 oz	50 g/2 oz	100 g/4 oz	200 g/7 oz
white grapes	300 g/11 oz	600 g/1¼ lb	1.2 kg/2½ lb	2.4 kg/4¾ lb
dry white wine	100 ml/3½ fl oz	200 ml/7 fl oz	400 ml/14 fl oz	800 ml/1 pint 8 fl oz
egg yolks	2	4	8	16
single cream	75 ml/3 fl oz	150 ml/¼ pint	300 ml/½ pint	600 ml/1 pint

Set oven at moderately hot (190 C, 375 F, gas 5).

Buy the fish skinned and filleted but reserve the skin and bones for making a court bouillon (see pages 32–3). Wipe and trim the fillets, add trimmings to the court bouillon. Leave to simmer.

Rub the fillets with lemon juice to flavour and whiten them. Season them with salt and freshly ground black pepper. Spread the butter on the base of a baking dish. Roll each fillet round your index finger, starting from the tail, skinned side outwards. Arrange the rolled fillets in the dish, packing them closely so that they will not unroll during cooking, or tie them with thick cotton which must be removed when serving.

Slit, but do not halve the grapes, and remove the seeds. Fill the centre of each rolled fillet with grapes and arrange the rest around. Pour in the wine. Strain the court bouillon and add enough to come half way up the turbans of fish. Lay a greased paper over the dish and poach the fish in the heated oven for 20 minutes or until white curd appears, showing that the fish is cooked. Remove the turbans to the heated serving dish and keep warm.

Boil the fish liquid until reduced by half. Beat the egg yolks and cream together and strain in 175 ml/6 fl oz of reduced fish liquid to every 2 egg yolks. Pour into a double boiler or a bowl over a pan of simmering water. Stir with a wooden spoon until the sauce coats the back of the spoon like a thin cream – do not overheat or the sauce will curdle. Taste and adjust the seasoning with lemon, salt and pepper. Pour the sauce round the fish. Keep warm or reheat in a bain-marie in the oven. Serve hot with Duchess potatoes.

If you are serving this as a first course allow one turban per person.

FLORENTINE-STYLE FILLETS OF SOLE

These sole fillets can be served in small portions as a first course or in the quantities given below as a main course for lunch. Either lemon or Dover sole may be used.

No. of servings	6	12	24	48
court bouillon (page 33)	150 ml/¼ pint	300 ml/½ pint	600 ml/1 pint	1.2 litres/2¼ pints
sole fillets, skinned (100 g/4 oz each)	12	24	48	96
lemon, to season	to taste	to taste	to taste	to taste
salt and pepper	to taste	to taste	to taste	to taste
CHEESE SAUCE				
butter	50 g/2 oz	100 g/4 oz	200 g/7 oz	400 g/14 oz
flour	50 g/2 oz	100 g/4 oz	200 g/7 oz	400 g/14 oz
milk	400 ml/14 fl oz	800 ml/1¼ pints	1.6 litres/2¾ pints	3.2 litres/5½ pints
cheddar cheese, grated	50 g/2 oz	100 g/4 oz	200 g/7 oz	400 g/14 oz
salt and pepper	to taste	to taste	to taste	to taste
spinach, frozen leaf	500 g/1 lb	1 kg/2¼ lb	2 kg/4¼ lb	4 kg/9 lb
butter	25 g/1 oz	50 g/2 oz	100 g/4 oz	200 g/7 oz
topping cheese	50 g/2 oz	100 g/4 oz	200 g/7 oz	400 g/14 oz

GARNISH *canned red pimento strips*

Set the oven at moderately hot (190 C, 375 F, gas 5).

Make court bouillon with bones from the fish (see page 33). Wipe fillets, season with lemon, salt and pepper and fold over in half. Arrange close together in a baking dish. Add court bouillon cover with foil and place in heated oven and poach for 10–15 minutes. Remove and drain carefully. Reduce the fish liquid to 100 ml/3¼ fl oz per 6 portions, strain and reserve.

To make the sauce: melt the butter, blend in the flour off the heat, then add the reduced fish liquid and milk. Bring to the simmer, stirring steadily and cook for 3 minutes. Remove from the heat and stir in the cheese until melted. Season.

To make the spinach: melt the butter, add spinach, cover and cook slowly for 15 minutes or until defrosted and cooked. Drain and press out all the liquid. Chop coarsely and season with salt and pepper.

Butter individual gratin dishes, and spoon spinach into each one. Place 2 fillets on top, coat with sauce. Top with grated cheese, brown in a hot oven or under the grill. Garnish.

TROUT STUFFED WITH HAZELNUTS AND HERBS

Rainbow trout baked with chervil or fennel makes a delightful lunch dish, especially in summer when fresh herbs are available. The delicate aniseed flavour of fennel has a special affinity with fish.

No. of servings	6	12	24	48
rainbow trout (200–250 g/7–8 oz each)	6	12	24	48
STUFFING				
hazelnuts	50 g/2 oz	100 g/4 oz	200 g/7 oz	400 g/14 oz
butter	25 g/1 oz	50 g/2 oz	100 g/4 oz	222 g/7 oz
shallots, finely chopped	1	2	4	8
fresh white breadcrumbs	50 g/2 oz	100 g/4 oz	200 g/7 oz	400 g/14 oz
chervil or fennel, fresh	2 tablespoons	4 tablespoons	8 tablespoons	50 g/2 oz
dried	2 teaspoons	4 teaspoons	2 tablespoons	4 tablespoons
grated lemon rind	1 teaspoon	2 teaspoons	4 teaspoons	2 tablespoons
salt and pepper	to taste	to taste	to taste	to taste
eggs, beaten	1	2	4	8
butter for greasing	40 g/1½ oz	50 g/2 oz	100 g/4 oz	200 g/7 oz
single cream	150 ml/¼ pint	300 ml/½ pint	600 ml/1 pint	1.2 litres/2¼ pints
lemon juice	1 tablespoon	2 tablespoons	4 tablespoons	8 tablespoons

GARNISH *fresh chervil or fennel or lemon wedges and parsley*

Scale the trout and clean them thoroughly. Trim off the fins. To prepare the stuffing: roast the hazelnuts under the grill or in a hot oven until the skins split. Rub off the skins and chop the nuts fairly coarsely. Mix with the breadcrumbs, herbs and lemon rind.

Heat the butter, fry the shallots until softened and mix into the stuffing. Season well with salt and freshly ground pepper and bind with the beaten eggs. Stuff trout, drawing the edges of the belly neatly together and securing them with skewers.

Set the oven at moderately hot (190 c, 375 f, gas 5).

Generously butter a baking tin and arrange the trout head to tail. Cover with a buttered paper and bake in the heated oven for 25–30 minutes according to size.

Warm a serving dish and place the cooked fish on it. Add the cream and the lemon juice to the baking tin, heat gently and pour it over the fish.

Garnish with fresh chervil or fennel sprigs or with lemon wedges and parsley and serve at once with new potatoes or pommes château.

TURBOT DUGLÉRE

ILLUSTRATED ON PAGES 126–7

The delicious sauce in this fish dish is named after its creator, the famous chef of the Old Café Anglais in Paris. It is equally suitable for other large high quality fish with firm white flesh like halibut, brill or bass, which can be cut across into steaks and boned. Make sure to get the head and trimmings for making the court bouillon. The dish can be made in advance and refrigerated or frozen.

No. of servings	6	12	24	48
court bouillon (page 32)	500 ml/17 fl oz	1 litres/1¾ pints	2 litres/3½ pints	3.5 litres/6 pints
turbot steaks (about 175 g/6 oz each)	6	12	24	48
lemon	1	2	3	4
salt and ground pepper	to taste	to taste	to taste	to taste
butter	25 g/1 oz	50 g/2 oz	75 g/3 oz	150 g/5 oz
shallots or small onion, chopped	2	4	8	12
fines herbes: fresh parsley, chervil, chives and thyme, chopped	1 teaspoon	2 teaspoons	4 teaspoons	8 teaspoons
dry white wine	225 ml/7½ fl oz	450 ml/¾ pint	900 ml/1½ pints	1.8 litres/ 3 pints
SAUCE				
tomatoes, firm, ripe	75 g/3 oz	150 g/5 oz	300 g/11 oz	600 g/1¼ lb
butter, unsalted	50 g/2 oz	100 g/4 oz	200 g/7 oz	400 g/14 oz
flour	50 g/2 oz	100 g/4 oz	200 g/7 oz	400 g/14 oz
single cream	60 ml/2½ fl oz	120 ml/scant 4 fl oz	240 ml/7½ fl oz	480 ml/16 fl oz
parsley, chopped	1 tablespoon	2 tablespoons	25 g/1 oz	50 g/2 oz
salt and pepper	to taste	to taste	to taste	to taste
lemon	to taste	to taste	to taste	to taste

Make the court bouillon using the fish heads and trimmings (see page 32). Wash and trim the steaks. Rub them with lemon juice and season to taste. Set the oven at moderately hot (190 c, 375 f, gas 5).

Generously butter a baking dish, cover the base with the shallots and sprinkle with the fines herbes. Arrange the steaks on top. Add the wine and enough court bouillon to come half way up the fish. Cover with greaseproof paper and poach in the heated oven for 20 minutes or until cooked. When white curds appear the fish is cooked.

Meanwhile, skin the tomatoes. Cut the flesh into julienne strips and sieve the pulp, reserving the juice. When the fish is cooked, remove it to a heated serving dish and keep it warm.

To make the sauce: rapidly boil the fish liquid to reduce it to 400 ml/14 fl oz for every 6 steaks. Melt the butter and off the heat stir in the flour to make a smooth roux. Gradually blend in the strained fish liquid and the tomato juice. Bring to the simmer, add the tomato juliennes and cook gently, stirring, for 5 minutes. Stir in the cream and the chopped parsley. Adjust the seasoning and sharpen with lemon juice. Pour over the fish and serve with new potatoes or surround with a border of Duchess potatoes or rice.

SMOKED HADDOCK KEDGEREE

This is a good dish to serve for brunch or breakfast after a late night. Smoked cod fillets can be used instead of haddock. It does not freeze very successfully, but it can be prepared in advance and refrigerated. When reheating, cook once to warm, or add melted butter or single cream so it will not be dry.

No. of servings	6	12	24	48
smoked haddock fillets, poached	400 g/14 oz	800 g/1¾ lb	1.6 kg/3½ lb	3.2 kg/7 lb
butter or margarine	100 g/4 oz	200 g/7 oz	400 g/14 oz	800 g/1¾ lb
rice, boiled	350 g/12 oz	700 g/1½ lb	1.4 kg/3 lb	2.8 kg/6 lb
hard-boiled egg, chopped	2	4	6	12
parsley, chopped	25 g/1 oz	50 g/2 oz	100 g/4 oz	225 g/8 oz
single cream (optional)	75 ml/3 fl oz	150 ml/¼ pint	300 ml/½ pint	600 ml/1 pint
lemon juice	to taste	to taste	to taste	to taste
salt and pepper	to taste	to taste	to taste	to taste

GARNISH *chopped parsley; hard-boiled egg white and sieved yolk; lemon twists*

Remove the skin and bones from the fish and flake it. Heat the butter and mix in the cooked rice and then the fish, the chopped hard-boiled egg and the parsley. Amalgamate all the ingredients well, sharpen with lemon juice and season generously with freshly ground black pepper. Taste and add salt if necessary. Turn into a warmed serving dish and smooth the top. Decorate with lines of chopped parsley and sieved yolk and chopped white of hard-boiled egg. Garnish with lemon twists. Serve with buttered green beans or petit pois à la françaises.

BAKED HADDOCK WITH MUSHROOM STUFFING

The shoulder steaks of large haddock, cod or hake are best for this dish. They should be cut about 2.5-cm/1-in thick. When cooked they freeze very successfully and if you add a little extra cider they can easily be reheated in the oven.

No. of servings	6	12	24	48
haddock steaks (about 150 g/5 oz each)	6	12	24	48
lemon	$\frac{1}{2}$	1	2	4
butter, for greasing dish				
salt and pepper	to taste	to taste	to taste	to taste
STUFFING				
butter	40 g/1½ oz	80 g/3 oz	160 g/5½ oz	320 g/11 oz
mushrooms, chopped	75 g/3 oz	150 g/5 oz	300 g/11 oz	600 g/1¼ lb
onion, chopped	25 g/1 oz	50 g/2 oz	100 g/4 oz	200 g/7 oz
rice, cooked	75 g/3 oz	150 g/5 oz	300 g/11 oz	600 g/1¼ lb
parsley, chopped	1 tablespoon	2 tablespoons	25 g/1 oz	50 g/2 oz
grated lemon rind	1 teaspoon	2 teaspoons	4 teaspoons	2 tablespoons
dried breadcrumbs	40 g/1½ oz	80 g/3 oz	160 g/5½ oz	320 g/11 oz
or grated cheese	50 g/2 oz	100 g/4 oz	200 g/7 oz	400 g/14 oz
mushroom caps	6	12	24	48
tomatoes, halved	6	12	24	48
cider or white wine	125 ml/4 fl oz	250 ml/8 fl oz	500 ml/17 fl oz	1 litre/1¾ pints
butter, for dotting				
GARNISH lemon twists and parsley				

Cut the fins off the fish, remove the backbone and other bones. Rub the top of the steaks with lemon juice. Butter a baking dish and place the steaks in it, season them with salt and freshly ground pepper. Prepare the stuffing: melt the butter and fry the chopped mushrooms and onion in it lightly. Mix in the rice, parsley and lemon rind. Season with salt and freshly ground pepper. Set the oven at moderately hot (200 c, 400 f, gas 6). Fill the cavities in the steaks with this mixture. Cover the fish, not the stuffing, with breadcrumbs, or grated cheese.

Place a mushroom cap on the stuffing in each steak and season. Halve the tomatoes, arrange them around the fish and season. Dot the fish and the vegetables with butter.

Pour in the cider. Cover the dish with greaseproof paper, place in the heated oven and bake for 45 minutes or until cooked.

Serve garnished with lemon twists and parsley. Jacket potatoes can be baked in the oven at the same time and make a good accompaniment for a hearty meal.

MACKEREL BAKED IN FOIL WITH CIDER

This is a tasty and handy way of cooking whole fish for outdoor meals. They can either be cooked on a barbecue or baked in an oven indoors and taken into the garden. Several other fish such as herring, fresh pilchards, trout and mullet can also be baked in the same way. Buy fish weighing about 250g/9oz each and allow one per person.

No. of servings	6	12	24	48
mackerel (about 250g/9oz each)	6	12	24	48
oil or melted butter	75g/3oz	150g/5oz	300g/11oz	600g/1½lb
salt and pepper	to taste	to taste	to taste	to taste
tomatoes, skinned	450g/1lb	900g/2lb	1.8kg/4lb	3.6kg/8lb
onion, finely chopped	75g/3oz	150g/5oz	300g/11oz	600g/1½lb
dried basil or thyme	2 teaspoons	4 teaspoons	8 teaspoons	2 tablespoons
mushroom caps	150g/5oz	300g/11oz	600g/1½lb	1kg/2¾lb
cider	100ml/4floz	200ml/7floz	400ml/14floz	800ml/1½ pints

GARNISH *fresh fennel or parsley and lemon wedges*

Scale and clean the fish. Cut off the fins and head if desired. Cut foil squares about 30 × 30cm/12 × 12in and brush them with oil or melted butter. Place each fish on half of the square. Brush with oil or butter and season well. Cover with a sliced tomato and a tablespoon of chopped onion. Sprinkle with basil or thyme and season. Arrange mushroom caps round each fish, dividing them equally between all the fish. Set the oven at hot (220c, 425f, gas 7). Season and drizzle oil or butter over the fish and vegetables. Add a tablespoon of cider to each serving. Fold the other half of the foil over the fish and roll the edges firmly together. Put the packets in a roasting tin and place in the heated oven. Bake for 30–40 minutes, or on a barbecue grid and grill, turning once.

When serving, open the foil slightly and insert a wedge of lemon and a sprig of fresh fennel or parsley. Serve with baked jacket potatoes or crusty French bread or rolls.

Jura-style Cold Trout

This dish can be served hot, but it is often more convenient to serve it cold. For a first course use small trout, but for a main course they should weigh about 250g/9oz each.

No. of servings	6	12	24	48
trout (about 250g/9oz each)	6	12	24	48
butter	50g/2oz	75g/3oz	150g/5oz	300g/11oz
shallots	2	4	8	16
salt and black pepper	to taste	to taste	to taste	to taste
dry white wine	150ml/$\frac{1}{4}$ pint	300ml/$\frac{1}{2}$ pint	600ml/1 pint	1.2 litres/2$\frac{1}{4}$ pints
HOLLANDAISE SAUCE				
egg yolks	3	5	9	18
lemon juice	1 tablespoon	2 tablespoons	4 tablespoons	120ml/4floz
unsalted butter	100g/4oz	200g/7oz	400g/14oz	800g/1$\frac{3}{4}$lb
reduced fish liquid	4 tablespoons	120ml/4floz	240ml/7$\frac{1}{2}$floz	480ml/16floz
double cream	25ml/1floz	50ml/2floz	100ml/4floz	200ml/7floz
GARNISH cucumber and capers				

Set the oven at cool (150c, 300f, gas 2).

Clean and scale the trout, leaving on the head. Butter a baking dish and lay the fish in it.

Peel and chop shallots, scatter over fish. Season. Pour in the wine and cover dish with a greased piece of paper. Bake for 25–30 minutes.

Meanwhile, make the hollandaise sauce (see page 184), using the egg yolks, lemon juice and butter.

When the fish are cooked, skin them carefully. Remove backbone. Slit down the back, then cut through bone with pointed scissors behind gills and just above tail. Ease out with tweezers. Arrange fish on a serving plate, cool.

Strain the fish liquid and reduce it by boiling rapidly to 4 tablespoons for every 6 fish. Cool, stir into hollandaise sauce. Gradually add cream, adjust seasoning. Sharpen to taste with lemon juice. Coat the trout with sauce.

To decorate: slice unpeeled cucumber, cut the slices into narrow strips. Arrange down trout in a herringbone pattern and put a caper in between each V, and in the eye sockets.

CHAUDFROID OF SALMON TROUT

ILLUSTRATED ON PAGES 46–7

This is an impressive dish for an elegant cold buffet. Salmon trout can vary in weight from 500 g/1 lb to 4 kg/9 lb and many people consider its texture to be finer than salmon.
For the chaudfroid sauce use the poaching liquid from the fish.
The fish and sauce should be cooked one day ahead but the coating and decorating should be done on the day. The dish cannot be frozen. The aspic can be made with jelly crystals and can be flavoured with white wine.

No. of servings	6	12	24	48
salmon trout	1 × 1.5 kg/3½ lb	1 × 3 kg/6¾ lb	2 × 3 kg/6½ lb	4 × 3 kg/6½ lb
court bouillon (page 33)	1 litre/1¾ pints	1.5 litres/2¾ pints	3 litres/5½ pints	5 litres/8¾ pints
capers	2	2	4	8
CHAUDFROID SAUCE				
velouté of fish (pages 186)	1 litre/1¾ pints	2 litres/3½ pints	4 litres/7 pints	8 litres/14 pints
aspic jelly	250 ml/8 fl oz	.5 litre/17 fl oz	1 litre/1¾ pints	2 litres/3½ pints
lemon juice	to taste	to taste	to taste	to taste
salt	to taste	to taste	to taste	to taste

GARNISH *watercress sprigs, chervil or lettuce leaves; or radish roses; sliced cucumber; tomato lilies*

Set the oven at moderately hot (190 C, 325 F, gas 3).

The fishmonger should scale and gut the salmon trout, but it will still be necessary to clean it thoroughly, scraping and washing out any blood which clings to the backbone.

Place the fish in a large roasting pan and cover with hot court bouillon. Cover the tin with buttered foil and poach in the heated oven for 30–50 minutes, taking care not to overcook. Take off the foil and allow the fish to cool in the liquid. Remove and carefully peel off the skin. Slit the fish along the back and snip the backbone with scissors just behind the head and above the tail. With tweezers carefully extract the backbone in one piece. Remove the eyes and replace with capers. Place the fish on a rack over a large clean dish.

Heat the velouté sauce, whisking in the liquid aspic and simmer until reduced to a coating consistency, it should just coat the back of a wooden spoon. Adjust the seasoning with lemon and salt. Ladle evenly over the fish and chill until set. Remove the rack with the fish, collect the surplus sauce and clean the dish. Replace the fish on the rack over a dish. Pour some aspic into a small dish, dip in each prawn and arrange down centre of fish.

Cool the remaining liquid aspic in a bowl of iced water until tacky and syrupy, spoon this carefully over the fish until completely glazed.

When firmly set, move the fish to the serving dish and garnish with chervil. Serve any extra sauce separately. Accompany with green salad and potato or rice salad (see page 142).

RUSSIAN FISH PIE

ILLUSTRATED ON PAGE 35

This is a very versatile recipe. You can either use rough puff or flaky pastry. The filling can be any fresh white fish, haddock, cod, hake or smoked fillets as below.

No. of servings	6	12	24	48
smoked haddock or cod fillet	500 g/1 lb 2 oz	1 kg/2¼ lb	2 kg/4½ lb	4 kg/9 lb
butter	40 g/1½ oz	80 g/3 oz	160 g/5½ oz	320 g/11 oz
mushrooms, sliced	225 g/8 oz	450 g/1 lb	900 g/2 lb	1.8 kg/4 lb
shallots or small onions, finely sliced	2	4	8	16
flour	40 g/1½ oz	80 g/3 oz	160 g/5½ oz	320 g/11½ oz
half milk and half fish liquid	200 ml/7 fl oz	400 ml/14 fl oz	800 ml/1¼ pints	1.6 litres/2¾ pints
parsley, chopped	2 tablespoons	25 g/1 oz	50 g/2 oz	100 g/4 oz
lemon juice	1 tablespoon	2 tablespoons	4 tablespoons	7–8 tablespoons
freshly ground pepper	to taste	to taste	to taste	to taste
hard-boiled eggs (optional)	2	4	8	16
pastry, rough puff (see page 187) or frozen puff pastry	575 g/1¼ lb	1.1 kg/3 lb	2.3 kg/6 lb	4.6 kg/12 lb
egg, for glazing	1	2	3	6
milk, for glazing	1 tablespoon	2 tablespoons	3 tablespoons	90 ml/3 fl oz

GARNISH *lemon crescents and parsley sprigs*

Put the smoked fish in cold water, bring to the simmer and cook very gently for 10 minutes. Drain and reserve the cooking liquid. Flake the fish coarsely, discarding the skin and any bones.

Melt the butter and fry the sliced mushrooms and onion in it until softened, but do not allow them to colour. Withdraw from the heat and stir in the flour to make a smooth roux. Mix the milk and fish liquid in equal quantities and blend into the roux. Return to the heat and bring to the simmer, stirring steadily. Cook gently for 5 minutes. Add the parsley and season to taste with lemon juice and freshly ground pepper. As smoked fish is generally salted, additional salt is not usually needed. Set the oven at hot (220 C, 425 F, gas 7).

Mix in the flaked fish and chopped hard-boiled egg, if used, and spread out this filling to cool. Roll the pastry out thinly into a rectangle slightly bigger than 30 × 50 cm/12 × 20 in. For 6 individual pies cut out 6 × 15-cm/6-in squares. Put 2 tablespoons of filling in each centre. Mix the egg and milk together to make a wash. Brush the pastry edges with this wash, fold the corners to meet in the centre. Overlap the edges and press down or they will open during baking. Leave the outer corners open for the steam to escape. Work up the trimmings and with hors d'oeuvres pastry cutters, cut out shapes. Brush the pies with the egg wash, put the shapes on pies. Glaze with the egg wash. Lift onto a greased baking sheet. Place in the heated oven and bake for 20 minutes or until well risen and golden brown. Serve hot, garnished with lemon crescents and parsley sprigs.

FISH CHOWDER

An ideal winter warmer. You can use prawns instead of crab meat.

No. of servings	6	12	24	48
cod fillet, fresh or smoked	450 g/1 lb	900 g/2 lb	1.8 kg/4 lb	3.6 kg/8 lb
pickled pork belly	75 g/3 oz	150 g/6 oz	300 g/12 oz	600 g/1½ lb
butter	25 g/1 oz	50 g/2 oz	100 g/4 oz	225 g/8 oz
potatoes, cubed	225 g/8 oz	450 g/1 lb	900 g/2 lb	1.8 kg/4 lb
onion, chopped	100 g/4 oz	225 g/8 oz	450 g/1 lb	900 g/2 lb
mushrooms, sliced	50 g/2 oz	100 g/4 oz	225 g/8 oz	450 g/1 lb
flour	25 g/1 oz	50 g/2 oz	100 g/4 oz	225 g/8 oz
milk	300 ml/½ pint	600 ml/1 pint	1.2 ml/2 pints	2.4 ml/4 pints
reserved liquid	450 ml/¾ pints	900 ml/1½ pints	1.8 ml/3 pints	3.6 ml/ 6 pints
white crab meat, flaked	50 g/2 oz	100 g/4 oz	225 g/8 oz	450 g/1 lb
salt and black pepper	to taste	to taste	to taste	to taste
lemon juice	to taste	to taste	to taste	to taste

GARNISH *minced fresh parsley; croûtons*

Wash the fish and cut it into pieces. Put it in a saucepan and cover it with water. Bring to the boil and simmer for 10 minutes. Drain the fish and reserve the liquid. Remove the rind and gristle from the pork and dice it. Melt the butter. Fry the pork slowly in it until crisp, add the potatoes, onion and mushrooms and fry for 5 minutes. Remove the pan from the heat and stir in the flour, then gradually add the milk and the reserved liquid. Add the fish (which will break up in cooking) and the flaked crab meat. Simmer for 10 minutes. Season cautiously as pork and smoked fish are already salty. Add lemon juice to taste and garnish.

STEAMED FISH SOUFFLÉ WITH BERCY SAUCE

ILLUSTRATED ON PAGE 97

This soufflé can be made with haddock, cod or whiting fillets. Because it is steamed, it does not collapse as quickly as other hot soufflés and will wait for the tardy guest. You can either cook it in individual soufflé dishes or in one large dish for 6 portions. The Bercy sauce (see page 186) is made with onion, the fish liquid, white wine and cream.

No. of servings	6	12	24	48
court bouillon (page 33), about	1.5 litres/2¾ pints	2 litres/3½ pints	4 litres/7 pints	8 litres/14 pints
haddock fillets smoked or fresh	750 g/1½ lb	1.5 kg/3¼ lb	3 kg/6½ lb	6 kg/13 lb
butter	40 g/1½ oz	80 g/3 oz	160 g/5½ oz	320 g/11½ oz
flour	40 g/1½ oz	80 g/3 oz	160 g/5½ oz	320 g/11½ oz
milk	125 ml/4 fl oz	250 ml/8 fl oz	500 ml/17 fl oz	1 litres/1¾ pints
fish liquid	125 ml/4 fl oz	250 ml/8 fl oz	500 ml/17 fl oz	1 litre/1¾ pints
eggs, separated	3	6	12	24
single cream	125 ml/4 fl oz	250 ml/8 fl oz	500 ml/17 fl oz	1 litre/1¾ pints
salt and pepper	to taste	to taste	to taste	to taste
lemon juice	to taste	to taste	to taste	to taste
anchovy essence	1–2 teaspoons	2–4 teaspoons	1 tablespoon	2 tablespoons
parsley, chopped	2 tablespoons	25 g/1 oz	50 g/2 oz	100 g/4 oz

GARNISH *parsley, chopped*

Put sufficient court bouillon in a large saucepan to cover the fish and bring it to the boil. Wipe and trim the fish and put it into the simmering court bouillon. If you are using smoked fish put it into cold water instead of into a court bouillon. Simmer gently, uncovered, for 10 minutes or until cooked.

Set the oven at moderately hot (190 c, 375 f, gas 5).

Lift out the fish, remove the skin and any bones and flake it finely with a fork or purée it. Reserve the cooking liquid for the sauce. Make a binding sauce by melting the butter, adding the flour to make a smooth roux. Add the milk and strained fish liquid and cook for 5 minutes. Beat the egg yolks with the cream and gradually stir into the sauce. Mix in the pepper, lemon juice and anchovy essence. Add the chopped parsley. Whisk egg whites until stiff but not dry and fold into the mixture.

For every six servings, grease a 15-cm/6-in soufflé dish, tie a band of greaseproof paper round the outside, standing 5 cm/2 in above the rim. Prepare a bain-marie for the oven by pouring 2 cm/$\frac{3}{4}$ in of water in a roasting tin. Pour the fish mixture into the soufflé dish, place in the heated oven and bake for 45 minutes or until set.

Place on a serving dish, garnish the top of the soufflé with chopped parsley. Serve immediately with Bercy sauce (see page 186).

FRESH SARDINES BRATHERINGE

These tasty little fish which have always been popular on the continent are now readily available in Britain. They make an excellent first course, grilled or fried, but are more convenient for larger parties if fried and then marinated as in this German recipe, as they can be prepared in advance.

No. of servings	6	12	24	48
fresh sardines	500 g/1 lb 2 oz	1 kg/2$\frac{1}{4}$ lb	2 kg/4$\frac{1}{2}$ lb	4 kg/9 lb
flour, for coating				
vegetable oil, for frying				
MARINADE				
wine vinegar	200 ml/7 fl oz	400 ml/14 fl oz	800 ml/1$\frac{3}{4}$ pints	1.6 litres/3$\frac{1}{2}$ pints
water	100 ml/3$\frac{1}{2}$ fl oz	200 ml/7 fl oz	400 ml/14 fl oz	800 ml/1$\frac{1}{4}$ pints
olive oil	50 ml/2 fl oz	100 ml/3$\frac{1}{2}$ fl oz	200 ml/7 fl oz	400 ml/14 fl oz
black peppercorns	1 teaspoon	2 teaspoons	4 teaspoons	1$\frac{1}{2}$ tablespoons
mustard seeds	1 teaspoon	2 teaspoons	4 teaspoons	1$\frac{1}{2}$ tablespoons
bay leaves	2	3	6	8
onion	75 g/3 oz	150 g/5 oz	300 g/11 oz	600 g/1$\frac{1}{4}$ lb

Cut the heads off the sardines. Split them open down the belly and gut them. Open them flat, place them back upwards on a board and press your thumb firmly down the backbone. Turn them over and remove the backbone. Wash in cold water and dry. Flour lightly. Heat the oil and brown them in it. Drain, season with salt and arrange in a gratin dish. Mix all the marinade ingredients together in a pan. Bring to the boil and pour mixture over the sardines. Leave for at least 24 hours.

Remove the sardines from the marinade and fold each fish together again. Serve in individual dishes, allowing 2–3 per person according to size. Serve with thinly sliced brown bread and butter.

—————— VARIATION ——————

Choose small pilchards, usually 2 per person will be enough and prepare these in the same way.

PROVENÇALE-STYLE RED MULLET

ILLUSTRATED ON PAGE 156

Red mullet is a delicious fish and is available frozen. If you can buy it fresh its flavour is even better. You can also use grey mullet but as they are usually larger fish it may be better to fillet them into 150-g/5-oz portions. Fillets of cod, whiting or haddock also make a tasty dish.

No. of servings	6	12	24	48
red mullet (about 225–250 g/8–9 oz each)	6	12	24	48
olive oil, about	2 tablespoons	4 tablespoons	60 ml/2½ fl oz	120 ml/4 fl oz
onion, thinly sliced	225 g/8 oz	450 g/1 lb	900 g/2 lb	1.8 kg/4 lb
dry white wine	150 ml/¼ pint	300 ml/½ pint	600 ml/1 pint	1.2 litres/2¼ pints
canned Italian tomatoes	400 g/14 oz	800 g/1¾ lb	1.6 kg/3½ lb	3.2 kg/7 lb
court bouillon or light stock	300 ml/½ pint	600 ml/1 pint	1.2 litres/2¼ pints	2.4 litres/4¼ pints
garlic, clove, crushed	1 (large)	2	4	8
bay leaf	1	2	4	6
fennel seeds, crushed	½ teaspoon	1 teaspoon	2 teaspoons	4 teaspoons
basil, dried	½ teaspoon	1 teaspoon	2 teaspoons	4 teaspoons
oregano, dried	½ teaspoon	1 teaspoon	2 teaspoons	4 teaspoons
sugar	1 teaspoon	2 teaspoons	4 teaspoons	2 tablespoons
salt and pepper	to taste	to taste	to taste	to taste

GARNISH *small black olives; fresh fennel sprigs, or lemon twists and chopped fresh parsley*

Set the oven at moderately hot (200 C, 400 F, gas 6).

Scale and clean the fish, but do not remove the mullet liver. Heat the oil in a saucepan and fry the onions gently until softened. Add the wine and bubble for a few moments. Add the tomatoes, court bouillon, garlic and herbs. Season with the sugar, salt and pepper and cook for 10 minutes.

Oil a baking dish, put in the fish and pour over the tomato sauce. Place in the heated oven and bake until done, about 25 minutes. Remove the fish to a heated serving dish and keep warm.

Boil the sauce rapidly until thickened. Remove the bay leaf and put the sauce through a mouli-légumes or into a blender and purée. Reheat, adjust the seasoning and pour over the fish. Garnish with small black olives and sprigs of fresh fennel or lemon twists and chopped fresh parsley.

MEAT

This is usually considered the most important course in the menu. It is not a seasonal commodity although new season's home-produced lamb can be specially featured when available. When buying meat you need to allow about 120 g/5 oz of boneless meat for each portion, and 180–200 g/7–8 oz per portion on the bone.

FLEMISH CARBONNADE OF BEEF

ILLUSTRATED ON PAGE 138

Carbonnades is the Belgian word for the little steaks of beef casseroled in this tasty dish. Sometimes the mushrooms are omitted but the crunchy topping of sliced French bread spread with mustard is a characteristic feature and makes an interesting change from pastry.

No. of servings	6	12	24	48
topside or leg of beef	750 g/1¾ lb	1.5 kg/3¼ lb	3 kg/6½ lb	6 kg/13 lb
seasoned flour, for coating				
beef dripping	75 g/3 oz	150 g/5 oz	300 g/11 oz	600 g/1¼ lb
mushrooms, sliced	150 g/6 oz	300 g/11 oz	600 g/1¼ lb	1.2 kg/2½ lb
onions, sliced	250 g/8 oz	500 g/1 lb 1 oz	1 kg/2¼ lb	2 kg/4½ lb
brown sugar	20 g/¾ oz	40 g/1½ oz	80 g/3 oz	160 g/6 oz
brown ale	400 ml/14 fl oz	800 ml/1¼ pints	1.8 litres/2¾ pints	3.1 litres/5¼ pints
brown stock, about	500 ml/17 fl oz	1 litre/1¾ pints	2.2 litres/4 pints	4.4 litres/8 pints
salt and black pepper	to taste	to taste	to taste	to taste
French bread, about	½ short loaf	1 short loaf	1 long loaf	2 long loaves
French mustard, about	75 g/3 oz	150 g/6 oz	300 g/11 oz	600 g/1¼ lb
butter or margarine about	50 g/2 oz	100 g/4 oz	200 g/7 oz	400 g/14 oz

Slice the meat into small steaks about 4 cm/1¾ in wide and 1.5 cm/¾ in thick. Coat with seasoned flour. Heat the dripping in a pan and quickly brown the steaks on both sides in the sizzling hot fat. Remove from the pan. Fry the mushrooms and onions in the same fat, stirring well until golden. Replace the meat. Add the brown sugar and beer and enough stock just to cover the meat. Bring to the boil and season to taste. Pour into a shallow casserole, cover closely with either a tight fitting lid or foil, put into the heated oven and simmer gently for 1½ hours until the meat is nearly cooked.

Set the oven at moderate (160 c, 325 f, gas 3).

Cut the French bread into 2-cm/¾-in thick slices. Cream the French mustard – use the yellow not the brown type – with the butter and spread it fairly thickly on one side of each slice of bread. When the meat is tender, cover the casserole with the slices, mustard side upwards, turn up the heat to moderately hot, 200 c, 400 f, gas 6 and continue cooking for 15–20 minutes until the bread has soaked up the gravy underneath and has become crusty on top.

Moussaka (see page 77) and Jalebis (see page 176)

Curried Apple Soup (see page 41) and Chicken Paprika
(see page 110)

MOUSSAKA

ILLUSTRATED ON PAGE 75

*This dish can be varied. Minced lamb or beef can be used; courgettes can replace
aubergines. The topping can either be a cheese sauce, or a savoury custard.*

No. of servings	6	12	24	48
aubergines, sliced	500 g/1 lb 2 oz	1 kg/2¼ lb	2 kg/4½ lb	4 kg/9 lb
onions, sliced	500 g/1 lb 2 oz	1 kg/2¼ lb	2 kg/4½ lb	4 kg/9 lb
olive oil	4 tablespoons	100 ml/3¼ fl oz	200 ml/7 fl oz	400 ml/14 fl oz
butter	50 g/2 oz	100 g/4 oz	200 g/7 oz	400 g/14 oz
minced lean beef or lamb	500 g/1 lb 2 oz	1 kg/2¼ lb	2 kg/4½ lb	4 kg/9 lb
red wine	100 ml/3¼ fl oz	200 ml/7 fl oz	400 ml/14 fl oz	800 ml/28 fl oz
canned tomatoes	400 g/14 oz	800 g/1¾ lb	1.6 kg/3½ lb	3.2 kg/7 lb
salt and pepper	to taste	to taste	to taste	to taste
sugar	2 teaspoons	4 teaspoons	40 g/1½ oz	80 g/3 oz
dried basil and oregano, mixed	½ teaspoon	1 teaspoon	2 teaspoons	4 teaspoons
Cheddar cheese, grated	40 g/1½ oz	80 g/3 oz	160 g/6 oz	320 g/11 oz
dried breadcrumbs	40 g/1½ oz	80 g/3 oz	160 g/6 oz	320 g/11 oz
CHEESE SAUCE				
butter	50 g/2 oz	100 g/4 oz	200 g/7 oz	400 g/14 oz
flour	50 g/2 oz	100 g/4 oz	200 g/7 oz	400 g/14 oz
milk	300 ml/½ pint	600 ml/1 pint	1.2 litres/2¼ pints	2.4 litres/4 pints
eggs, beaten	2	4	8	16
Cheddar cheese, grated	50 g/2 oz	100 g/4 oz	200 g/7 oz	400 g/14 oz

Blanche aubergine slices for 3 minutes in boiling water, drain. Heat oil, fry aubergine until golden. Fry onion in oil until softened. Add butter mix in minced meat and cook, stirring, until browned. Add wine and cook for 2–3 minutes. Stir in tomatoes. Season and add sugar, sprinkle in herbs. Set the oven at cool (150C, 300F, gas 2). Make a roux with the butter and flour, blend in milk, cook

2 minutes. Add a little sauce to the beaten eggs, blend into the sauce. Stir in the cheese. Season.

To assemble: lightly oil a deep gratin dish, put in alternate layers of aubergines and meat mixture, beginning and ending with aubergines. Spread the cheese sauce over. Mix together the extra grated cheese and breadcrumbs and sprinkle over sauce. Bake for 30–40 minutes until golden.

TOULOUSE-STYLE CASSOULET

ILLUSTRATED ON PAGE 58

To get all the flavours of this tasty peasant dish well blended it is best to cook it a day ahead of eating it and then reheat it, adding the crust at this stage.

No. of servings	12	24	48
haricot beans, soaked overnight in cold water	750 g/1¾ lb	1.5 kg/3¼ lb	3 kg/6½ lb
green forehock of bacon, lean	675 g/1½ lb	1.3 kg/2¾ lb	2.3 kg/5 lb
bouquet garni	1	2	4
onion, clouté (studded with cloves)	1	2	4
duckling, dressed weight (2 kg/4½ lb)	1	2	4
lamb, shoulder, boned	1.25 kg/2½ lb	2.5 kg/5½ lb	5 kg/11 lb
olive oil	4 tablespoons	100 ml/3½ fl oz	200 ml/7 fl oz
onion or shallots, finely chopped	500 g/1 lb 1½ oz	1 kg/2¼ lb	2 kg/4½ lb
celery, chopped	150 g/5 oz	300 g/11 oz	600 g/1¼ lb
canned tomatoes	600 g/1¼ lb	1.2 kg/2½ lb	2.4 kg/5½ lb
dried thyme	1¼ teaspoons	2½ teaspoons	5 teaspoons
garlic cloves	3	6	12
freshly ground black pepper	1 teaspoon	2 teaspoons	4 teaspoons
Toulouse sausage, cut into thick slices	375 g/13 oz	750 g/1½ lb	1.5 kg/3¼ lb
dried breadcrumbs	200 g/7 oz	400 g/14 oz	800 g/1¾ lb
parsley, chopped	1 tablespoon	2 tablespoons	4 tablespoons

Set the oven at hot (220c, 425f, gas 7).

Drain the beans and put them into a large pan with the hock, cover with fresh water and bring to the boil. Discard the water and cover with fresh water, add the bouquet garni and the onion studded with cloves. Simmer for about 1½ hours until the beans are almost cooked. Remove the hock and strain the beans reserving the liquid. Cut the rind off the hock and then cut into 2-cm/¾-in squares.

Place the duck in the heated oven and part roast it for 35–40 minutes. Remove from the oven, cool slightly. Divide each leg into 2 joints and cut the breast into neat pieces. Trim all the fat off the lamb and cut it into large pieces, brown it in olive oil. Add the chopped onion and celery, the tomatoes, herbs, garlic and pepper. Add enough of the reserved bean liquid to cover the meat. Simmer for about 45 minutes until the lamb is tender.

Reset the oven to cool (150 c, 300 f, gas 2). For 12 servings, use 2 large casseroles (2-litre/3-pint size) and put in a layer of beans and diced rind. On top of this put pieces of duck and gammon and half

the lamb with tomato mixture and half the sausage, cut into thick slices. Cover with beans, then the remaining meats and top with the remaining beans and add enough of the reserved bean liquid to come just below the surface. Cover with a lid and bake in the heated oven for 2 hours. Adjust the seasoning.

Next day, set the oven at moderate (180 c, 350 f, gas 4). Cover the cassoulet with a layer of breadcrumbs and place in the oven for 1–1½ hours until heated through and a crisp crust has formed on top. Garnish with chopped parsley.

PORK TENDERLOIN CAUCHOISE

This is a Normandy dish made from typical Normandy ingredients: cider, Calvados, butter and cream. If you use leg fillets you will need to allow a longer time.

No. of servings	6	12	24	48
pork tenderloin	900 g/2 lb	1.8 kg/4 lb	3.6 kg/8 lb	7.2 kg/16 lb
butter	100 g/4 oz	225 g/8 oz	450 g/1 lb	900 g/2 lb
onion, sliced	175 g/6 oz	350 g/12 oz	675 g/1½ lb	1.3 kg/3 lb
mushrooms, sliced	350 g/12 oz	675 g/1½ lb	1.3 kg/3 lb	2.7 kg/6 lb
dry cider	250 ml/8 fl oz	500 ml/17 fl oz	950 ml/1¾ pints	1.9 ml/scant 3½ pints
Calvados	75 ml/2½ fl oz	150 ml/¼ pint	250 ml/8 fl oz	500 ml/17 fl oz
soured cream	150 ml/¼ pint	300 ml/½ pint	600 ml/1 pint	1.2 ml/2 pints
salt and pepper	to taste	to taste	to taste	to taste

GARNISH *apple rings fried in butter*

Trim the tenderloin and cut it into 1.5-cm/½-inch thick slices. Heat half the butter and fry the meat in it until golden brown on both sides. Remove and keep warm and fry the onion in the same butter until just coloured. Fry the mushrooms in a separate pan in remaining butter and set aside. Add the cider to the onions and boil up and reduce liquid by nearly half. Add the Calvados and again

reduce the liquid slightly, then add the mushrooms and stir in the soured cream. Return the pork to the pan with any juice that has run out and cook gently for 5 minutes or until tender. Adjust the seasoning. Serve garnished with apple rings lightly browned in butter. Accompany with French beans or mange tout peas.

BAKED PORK CHOPS WITH APPLE AND NUT STUFFING

This is an excellent autumn or winter dish, especially if served with stuffed baked potatoes and buttered cabbage or Brussels sprouts. Either loin or neck chops are suitable, but not spare ribs.

No. of servings	6	12	24	48
pork chops	6	12	24	48
cashew nuts	75 g/3 oz	150 g/5½ oz	300 g/11 oz	600 g/1¼ lb
bread, sliced	125 g/4½ oz	250 g/8¾ oz	500 g/1 lb 2 oz	1 kg/2¼ lb
cooking apples	1	2	4	8
butter or margarine	25 g/1 oz	50 g/2 oz	100 g/4 oz	200 g/7 oz
celery, finely chopped	2 tablespoons	4 tablespoons	8 tablespoons	12 tablespoons
onion, finely chopped	2 tablespoons	4 tablespoons	8 tablespoons	12 tablespoons
salt and pepper	to taste	to taste	to taste	to taste
savory, chopped *fresh*	1 tablespoon	2 tablespoons	4 tablespoons	8 tablespoons
dried	½ teaspoon	1 teaspoon	2 teaspoons	4 teaspoons
lemon juice	to taste	to taste	to taste	to taste
dry cider	150 ml/¼ pint	300 ml/½ pint	600 ml/1 pint	1.2 litres/2¼ pints

GARNISH *fried dessert apple rings and celery*

Set oven at moderately hot (180 c, 350 f, gas 5).

Trim the fat off the chops. Cut a large gash from the outer edge of the bone to form a pocket. Chop the nuts coarsely. Remove crusts from bread and dice. Peel, core and chop apples. Heat the butter and fry the nuts until golden. Add the apple, celery and onion and cook until softened. Mix in the bread, seasoning, herbs and lemon juice, continue cooking until mixture binds together. Stuff the chops and secure them with small skewers or wooden toothpicks. Heat a little oil and sear the chops on both sides, turning once. Put in an ovenproof dish, add the cider and cook for 45 minutes to 1 hour, until tender.

Remove the skewers and garnish. Core the unpeeled dessert apples and cut in 1-cm/½-in thick slices. Fry until golden and place one on top of each chop with a tuft of fresh celery leaves in the centre.

PORK AND APPLE GUIZOT

ILLUSTRATED ON PAGE 168

Pork and apple are an excellent combination. This dish is quick to prepare and is hearty enough for cold winter days. It can be prepared in advance and put into the oven an hour before it is needed. The cooked dish freezes very successfully.

No. of servings	6	12	24	48
butter or margarine	75 g/3 oz	150 g/5 oz	300 g/11 oz	600 g/1¼ lb
cooking apples, peeled and sliced	150 g/5½ oz	300 g/11 oz	600 g/1¼ lb	1.2 kg/2½ lb
coriander seeds, crushed	2 teaspoons	4 teaspoons	2½ tablespoons	5 tablespoons
onion, chopped	150 g/5½ oz	300 g/11 oz	600 g/1¼ lb	1.2 kg/2½ lb
salt and black pepper	to taste	to taste	to taste	to taste
pork chops	6	12	24	48
dried breadcrumbs	60 g/2 oz	120 g/4 oz	240 g/8 oz	480 g/1 lb
Cheddar or Gruyère cheese, grated	60 g/2 oz	120 g/4 oz	240 g/8 oz	480 g/1 lb
dry cider, about	150 ml/¼ pint	300 ml/½ pint	600 ml/1 pint	1.2 litres/2 pints

GARNISH *fried apple rings*

Set the oven at moderately hot (200 c, 400 F, gas 6).

Take some of the butter and spread it over the base of a gratin dish and cover it with the apples. Sprinkle with coriander and scatter over the chopped onion. Season to taste with salt and freshly ground black pepper. Trim the fat off the chops and arrange them on top of the apple bed and season. Mix together the breadcrumbs and grated cheese and cover the chops. Dot with the remaining butter or melt the remaining butter and drizzle it over the topping. Pour in enough cider to come half way up the chops.

Lay a piece of kitchen foil over the dish. Place in the heated oven and bake for 45 minutes to 1 hour, until tender. Remove the foil for the last 20 minutes to allow the topping to become crisp and golden. Serve garnished with apple rings fried in butter.

— VARIATIONS —

Follow the above recipe but use veal chops instead of pork, sliced mushroom instead of apple and coriander and dry white wine in place of cider. Bake as for pork chops. Both pork and veal must be thoroughly cooked.

TAGLIATELLE ALLA BOLOGNESE

ILLUSTRATED ON PAGES 86–7

The beauty of this simple recipe is that it can either be served straight from the oven or it can be totally prepared in advance and reheated or frozen and reheated.

No. of servings	6	12	24	48
butter or margarine	40 g/1½ oz	80 g/3 oz	150 g/5 oz	300 g/10 oz
bacon or ham trimmings, chopped	40 g/1½ oz	80 g/3 oz	150 g/5 oz	300 g/10 oz
onion, chopped	50 g/2 oz	100 g/4 oz	200 g/7 oz	400 g/14 oz
celery, chopped	50 g/2 oz	100 g/4 oz	200 g/7 oz	400 g/14 oz
mushrooms, sliced	75 g/3 oz	150 g/5 oz	300 g/10 oz	600 g/1¼ lb
minced lean beef	350 g/12 oz	700 g/1½ lb	1.4 kg/3¼ lb	2.8 kg/6 lb
chicken livers, chopped (optional)	75 g/3 oz	150 g/5 oz	300 g/10 oz	600 g/1¼ lb
tomato purée	50 g/2 oz	100 g/4 oz	200 g/7 oz	400 g/14 oz
red wine	150 ml/¼ pint	300 ml/½ pint	600 ml/1 pint	1.2 litres/2¼ pints
stock or water, about	200 ml/7 fl oz	400 fl/14 fl oz	800 ml/1¼ pints	1.6 litres/2¾ pints
dried basil or marjoram	½ teaspoon	1 teaspoon	2 teaspoons	1 tablespoons
nutmeg	to taste	to taste	to taste	to taste
sugar	1 teaspoon	2 teaspoons	1 tablespoon	2 tablespoons
salt and pepper	to taste	to taste	to taste	to taste
cooking oil	½ tablespoon	½ tablespoon	½ tablespoon	½ tablespoon
tagliatelle	350 g/12 oz	700 g/1½ lb	1.4 kg/3¼ lb	2.8 kg/6 lb
cheddar or gruyère cheese, grated, about	175 g/6 oz	350 g/12 oz	700 g/1½ lb	1.4 kg/3 lb

To make the Bolognese sauce, melt the butter and fry the bacon, onion, celery and mushrooms until softened. Add the minced beef and the chicken livers and brown. Stir in the tomato purée and the red wine and bubble for a few minutes. Add the stock or water, herbs, nutmeg, sugar and seasoning. Bring to the boil, cover and simmer for 30–40 minutes.

Bring a large pan of salted water to the boil, add the oil and drop the tagliatelle into it. Cook briskly for 8–10 minutes until only just tender. Stir occasionally. (Avoid cooking more than 1.5 kg/3¼ lb of pasta at a time as it tends to stick together.) Drain thoroughly.

Set the oven at moderately hot (200 c, 400 f, gas 6).

Cover the base of a gratin dish with a layer of sauce, then a layer of pasta, then sauce, then cheese, continue in this order until all the ingredients are used up. End with a layer of cheese on top.

Place in the heated oven and bake for 15–20 minutes until the top has a golden crust. Alternatively, store in a refrigerator or freezer and bake when required.

Serve with a tossed green salad or Italian-style haricots verts (see page 134).

CALF'S LIVER AND MARSALA SAUCE

ILLUSTRATED ON PAGE 98

Calf's liver is delicious but tends to be expensive. A cheaper substitute is lamb's liver, which has a stronger taste but also works well in this recipe. Sweet sherry or Madeira may be used instead of Marsala. The dish looks attractive served in a golden border of Duchess potatoes. (A word of caution, never overcook liver or it will go tough.)

No. of servings	6	12	24	48
liver, calf's or lamb's, sliced	600 g/1¼ lb	1.2 kg/2¾ lb	2.4 kg/5¼ lb	4.8 kg/10½ lb
seasoned flour, for coating				
butter	75 g/3 oz	150 g/5 oz	300 g/11 oz	600 g/1¼ lb
onion, sliced thinly	100 g/4 oz	200 g/7 oz	400 g/14 oz	800 g/1¾ lb
mushrooms, sliced	150 g/5 oz	300 g/11 oz	600 g/1¼ lb	1.2 kg/2½ lb
Marsala	75 ml/3 fl oz	150 ml/¼ pint	300 ml/½ pint	600 ml/1 pint
dried mixed herbs	½ teaspoon	1 teaspoon	2 teaspoons	4 teaspoons
canned tomatoes	150 g/5½ oz	300 g/11 oz	600 g/1¼ lb	1.2 kg/2½ lb
soured cream	100 ml/4 fl oz	200 ml/7 fl oz	400 ml/14 fl oz	800 ml/1½ pints
salt and black pepper	to taste	to taste	to taste	to taste

Set the oven at moderate (160c, 325f, gas 3).

Remove any skin and veins from the liver and pass the slices through the seasoned flour. Pat off any loose flour. Melt the butter and sear the liver in it quickly until it is golden on both sides. It must still be pink inside when removed. Place in a baking dish. Using the same pan, fry the onion and mushrooms gently until softened. You may need to add some extra fat. Add the Marsala and allow the mixture to bubble for 2–3 minutes. Add the herbs, canned tomatoes and season to taste. Bring to a simmer and pour over the liver. Place in the heated oven and bake for 20–25 minutes. Arrange the sliced liver on a warmed serving dish and keep warm. Liquidise the sauce. Blend in the cream and reheat without boiling. Adjust the seasoning and pour over the liver.

Serve with Duchess or creamed potatoes and buttered Brussels sprouts or French beans.

*Cheese, Apple and Ham Quiche (see page 19) and
Risotto Espagnole (see page 23)*

OSSI BUCCHI

For this hearty Italian dish, the shin of veal is sawn into sections about 3 cm/1 in thick. Allow 2 per person. The marrow from bones may, when cooked be removed and mixed into the accompanying Risotto alla Milanese (see page 23).

No. of servings	6	12	24	48
shin of veal	1 kg/2¼ lb	2 kg/4½ lb	4 kg/9 lb	8 kg/18 lb
seasoned flour, for coating				
butter or margarine	75 g/3 oz	150 g/5 oz	300 g/11 oz	600 g/1¼ lb
onion, sliced	250 g/9 oz	500 g/1 lb 2 oz	1 kg/2¼ lb	2 kg/4½ lb
celery, chopped	50 g/2 oz	100 g/4 oz	200 g/7 oz	400 g/14 oz
wine, white	150 ml/¼ pint	300 ml/½ pint	600 ml/1 pint	1.1 litres/2 pints
young carrots	250 g/9 oz	500 g/1 lb 2 oz	1 kg/2¼ lb	2 kg/4½ lb
canned tomatoes	350 g/12 oz	700 g/1½ lb	1.4 kg/3 lb	2.8 kg/6 lb
dried basil	½ teaspoon	1 teaspoon	2 teaspoons	4 teaspoons
dried oregano	½ teaspoon	1 teaspoon	2 teaspoons	4 teaspoons
bay leaf	1	2	3	6
salt and pepper	to taste	to taste	to taste	to taste
white stock (page 32)	500 ml/17 fl oz	1 litre/1¾ pints	2 litres/3½ pints	4 litres/7 pints
GREMOLATA				
lemon rind, grated	½	1	2	4
parsley, chopped	2 tablespoons	25 g/1 oz	50 g/2 oz	100 g/4 oz
garlic, finely chopped	1 teaspoon	2 teaspoons	4 teaspoons	8 teaspoons

Trim the veal and, if necessary, tie into shape. Coat with seasoned flour. Melt butter and brown meat quickly on both sides. Remove from pan. Fry onions and celery in the same butter until they turn golden. Replace veal, arranging the pieces upright so that the marrow remains intact during cooking. Pour over the wine and let it bubble for 5 minutes. Add the carrots, slicing or cutting them into fingers if they are large, tomatoes and herbs. Add enough stock to half cover veal. Season. Set the oven at moderate (175 C, 350 F, gas 4). Cover and cook in oven for 2 hours or until tender. Remove bay leaf and string, place on a serving dish.

To make the gremolata: mix lemon rind, parsley and garlic together. Scatter over veal. Serve with Risotto alla Milanese.

SPICED NOISETTES OF LAMB

ILLUSTRATED ON PAGE 97

Noisettes are usually cut from the boned loin of lamb. If they are cut $3\,cm/1\frac{1}{4}\,in$ thick, they will weigh about $100\,g/4\,oz$ each. If they are cut from the boned best end, then they will be smaller, weighing about $75\,g/3\,oz$ each. In either case, normally two noisettes per serving are allowed. If the butcher is preparing the noisettes, get him to trim the fat off well.

No. of servings	6	12	24	48
noisettes of lamb	12	24	48	96
root vegetables, for stock				
MARINADE				
soy sauce	2 teaspoons	4 teaspoons	120 ml/4 fl oz	240 ml/8 fl oz
French mustard, mild	1 tablespoon	2 tablespoons	4 tablespoons	8 tablespoons
vinegar, cider or wine	2 tablespoons	4 tablespoons	120 ml/4 fl oz	240 ml/8 fl oz
wine, white or red	2 tablespoons	4 tablespoons	120 ml/4 fl oz	240 ml/8 fl oz
olive oil or salad oil	1 tablespoon	2 tablespoons	4 tablespoons	150 ml/$\frac{1}{4}$ pint
garlic cloves, large	1	2	4	8
root ginger, finely chopped	1 teaspoon	2 teaspoons	4 teaspoons	3 tablespoons
coriander seeds, crushed	1 teaspoon	2 teaspoons	4 teaspoons	3 tablespoons
bay leaves	2	3	4	10
dried thyme or rosemary	$\frac{1}{4}$ teaspoon	$\frac{1}{2}$ teaspoon	1 teaspoon	2 teaspoons
GARNISH sprigs of fresh herbs				

Set the oven at moderate (160c, 325f, gas 3).

Make the noisettes if not ready prepared – see note at end of recipe. Put the bones on to make stock (see page 32). Thoroughly mix the ingredients for the marinade and pour it over the noisettes. Leave for several hours, or if possible, overnight, turning occasionally.

Drain the noisettes and reserve the marinade. Dry the meat with kitchen paper. Grease a frying pan and sear the noisettes quickly in it until nicely browned on both sides, turning once. Arrange on a baking dish. Remove the bay leaves from the marinade and pour it over the noisettes. Deglaze the pan in which the noisettes were fried with stock and then pour this into the dish to half cover the noisettes, adding extra if necessary. Bake in the heated oven for 35–40 minutes until tender. Place the noisettes on a warmed serving dish. Skim the fat off the sauce, boil it up and reduce it slightly, adjusting the seasoning. Remove the string from the noisettes and pour the sauce over. Garnish with sprigs of fresh rosemary or other herbs.

NOTE: *To make noisettes: cut off the chump end of the loin. Remove the chine bone and skin. Fillet out the rib bones carefully, leaving the fillet intact. Trim off all surplus fat. Place loin, fat side down on board, cover with damp greaseproof paper and beat out the flesh so it will encircle the eye of the meat when rolled. Remove the paper and season the meat. Roll up tightly from the eye to the end of the flap. Secure with skewers at even intervals. Tie tightly with thin string at 3-cm/1¼-in intervals, starting 1.5 cm/¾ in from the end. Remove the skewers and slice the joint into equal sized portions between the strings. Flatten the noisettes slightly with the cutlet bat.*

DEVILLED LAMB CUTLETS

ILLUSTRATED ON PAGE 137

This is an ideal dish if you are short of preparation time. Chicken joints may be substituted for the lamb and both meats can be barbecued instead of oven cooked.

No. of servings	6	12	24	48
neck of lamb cutlets *large*	6	12	24	48
small	12	24	48	96
DEVIL SAUCE				
lemon juice	3 tablespoons	75 ml/3 fl oz	150 ml/$\frac{1}{4}$ pint	300 ml/$\frac{1}{2}$ pint
whipping cream	200 ml/7 fl oz	400 ml/14 fl oz	800 ml/1$\frac{1}{4}$ pints	1.5 litres/2$\frac{1}{2}$ pints
mango chutney	2 tablespoons	4 tablespoons	120 ml/4 fl oz	240 ml/9 fl oz
mushroom ketchup	1 tablespoon	2 tablespoons	3 tablespoons	6 tablespoons
Dijon mustard	1 tablespoon	2 tablespoons	3 tablespoons	6 tablespoons
soya sauce	2 tablespoons	4 tablespoons	100 ml/4 fl oz	200 ml/7 fl oz
tomato ketchup and *Worcestershire sauce*	to taste	to taste	to taste	to taste

GARNISH *sprigs of watercress*

Trim any surplus fat off the cutlets and scrape the ends of the rib bones clean.

Add the lemon juice to the cream and then mix in all the other ingredients. If time permits, marinate the cutlets in the sauce.

Place the cutlets on the grid of a barbecue or on a grill, brush with the sauce, cook and when nicely coloured, turn, brush with sauce again and cook on the other side. Spoon any surplus sauce over the cutlets when serving. Garnish with sprigs of watercress. Accompany with baked jacket potatoes and roasted peppers, which can be done at the same time as the cutlets (see below).

Roasted Green Peppers

Allow about half a green pepper per portion. Prepare the peppers in advance by splitting and removing the stalk, seeds and membrane. Cut in halves or quarters, according to how big they are, brush with oil and season with salt and pepper. Roast on the grid over the charcoal or under the grill turning once. Before serving, remove any loose charred skin.

Steamed Fish Soufflé (see page 70) with Bercy Sauce
(see page 186) and Spiced Noisettes of Lamb (see page 94)

Calf's Liver and Marsala Sauce (see page 83) and
Honeydew Melon Sorbet (see page 179)

Lamb Cutlets in Pastry

ILLUSTRATED ON PAGE 125

These cutlets wrapped in crisp flaky pastry can be served hot with vegetables or cold with salads. They are ideal for outdoor occasions as they can be held by the frill and eaten with the fingers.

No. of servings	6	12	24	48
best end of lamb, chined, giving 6 cutlets	1	2	4	8
salt	to taste	to taste	to taste	to taste
flaky or puff pastry, rough puff if frozen finished weight	450 g/1 lb	900 g/2 lb	1.8 kg/4 lb	3.6 kg/8 lb
redcurrant or mint jelly	6 tablespoons	175 g/6 oz	350 g/12 oz	700 g/1½ lb
eggs, beaten	1	2	4	8
milk	1 tablespoon	2 tablespoons	4 tablespoons	120 ml/scant 4 fl oz

GARNISH *fresh mint or parsley sprigs; cutlet frills*

Set oven at moderately hot (200 c, 400 f, gas 6).

Place the lamb in the heated oven and bake for 20–25 minutes. The juice should turn slightly pink when tested.

Cool the meat, remove the chine bone and divide it into cutlets. Trim off all the fat and any gristle. Scrape clean 3 cm/1 in off at the end of each cutlet bone.

For every 6 cutlets, roll out the pastry thinly into a rectangle. Place a trimmed cutlet on the nearest end, with the bare bone protruding beyond the pastry edge. Cut out a shape 2 cm/¾ in larger than the chop. Use this as a pattern to cut out 11 more.

Place a cutlet on 6 shapes and spread the top with redcurrant or mint jelly. Brush the pastry border with water, cover with another shape and press firmly together to seal well. Knock the edges up with the back of a knife or scallop. Grease a baking sheet and place the cutlets on it. Beat the egg and milk together and use this to glaze the cutlets. Cut 2 or 3 slits in the top for the steam to escape. Decorate with pastry leaves. Glaze with beaten egg and milk mixture.

Set the oven at hot (230 c, 450 f, gas 8) and when hot bake the cutlets for 15 minutes until well risen. Reduce the heat slightly, bake for a further 10–15 minutes until cooked and golden brown.

Put a frill on each cutlet bone and garnish with parsley sprigs. Serve Bercy sauce (see page 186) made from meat stock (see page 32), separately.

— VARIATION —

Instead of lamb cutlets, use beef, allowing one tournedos weighing 100 g/4 oz for each person. Tie into neat rounds, but do not lard. Sear quickly on both sides in hot butter, so they are still rare inside. When cold, remove the string and spread the tops with liver pâté. Cut the pastry into circles, 2 cm/¾ in larger than the steaks, 2 to each tournedos and wrap like cutlets. Glaze, decorate and bake in a similar way.

Serve with Bercy sauce.

MEAT ROASTING

Joint	Approx. weight whole	Preparation
BEEF		
Sirloin	10 kg/22 lb (44 portions)	Cut to required weight between ribs. Butcher should saw through chine bone to facilitate removal before carving. Remove thick sinew and tie into shape
Wing rib	4 kg/9 lb (18 portions)	As sirloin, or bone and roll
Fore rib	4 kg/9 lb (18 portions)	As wing rib
LAMB		
Leg	2 kg/4½ lb (10 portions)	Separate shank and place in roasting tin to brown gravy. Remove chump bone to facilitate carving. Tie or skewer thick end of joint
Shoulder	2 kg/4½ lb (8 portions)	Remove end of knuckle. Trim fat. Bone and roll for easy carving. Good stuffed with breadcrumbs, herbs or dried apricots
Loin	1 kg/2¼ lb (3 portions) small lamb (6 portions) large lamb	Ask butcher to remove chine bone or chop between joints. Skin and score fat in trellis
Best end	1.25 kg/2¾ lb (3 portions)	As loin. Remove end of blade bone from end chop
Breast	800 g/1¾ lb (2–3 portions)	Bone, trim fat, stuff and roll. Weigh after stuffing. Roll 2 or more together

Oven Temperature	Special Points	Accompaniments
220 c, 425 f, gas 7, 15 mins per 500 g/1 lb + 15 mins. 220 c, 425 f, gas 7 for 20 mins, then 190 c, 375 f, gas 5 for 20 mins per 500 g/1 lb	Underdone, usually preferred. Well done	Horseradish sauce, roast potatoes and parsnips, green vegetables, Yorkshire puddings, gravy
As sirloin	If boned and rolled, 5 mins longer per 500 g/1 lb	As sirloin
190 c, 375 f, gas 5. 20 mins per 500 g/1 lb. 25 mins per 500 g/1 lb	Fatter and less tender than wing rib. Underdone. Well done	As sirloin
200 c, 400 f, gas 6 for 20 mins, then 190 c, 375 f, gas 5 for 20 mins per 500 g/1 lb	Good lean joint	Mint or onion sauce, or red-currant jelly, roast potatoes, onions, green vegetables, peas
190 c, 375 f, gas 5. 20 mins per 500 g/1 lb	Good but less expensive than leg because fatter. If stuffed, 5 mins longer per 500 g/1 lb	As leg
As leg	Carve between ribs. Serve 2 small cutlets or 1 large per portion	As leg, plus country dumplings unless joint boned and stuffed
As leg	Carve between rib. Serve 2 cutlets per portion	As loin
190 c, 375 f, gas 5. 25 mins per 500 g/1 lb	Second quality meat but inexpensive	As loin

Joint	Approx. weight whole	Preparation
PORK		
Leg	5 kg/11¼ lb (25–28 portions)	To reduce cooking time, halve joint, remove trotter and score skin 5 mm/¼ in deep, approx. 1 cm/½ in apart. Brush with oil and sprinkle generously with salt to crisp crackling
Loin	6.5 kg/14½ lb (24–30 portions)	Can be cut to desired weight between ribs – ask butcher to remove chine. Alternatively, bone, spread with stuffing, then roll and tie. Weight after stuffing
Blade	1.5 kg/3½ lb (6–8 portions)	Bone, stuff and secure neatly. Score as leg and oil and salt
Hand and Spring	3 kg/6¾ lb (10–12 portions)	Remove trotter and surplus fat. Score as leg. Can be boned and rolled
Belly	2.75 kg/6 lb (10 portions)	Score, oil and salt as leg. Can be boned, stuffed and rolled
VEAL		
Leg, small	5–5.5 kg/11–12 lb (24 portions)	Can be halved. Spread with stuffing or streaky bacon
Loin	2.75 kg/6 lb (10–12 portions)	Chine or chop between ribs or bone, stuff and roll
Best end	3.25 kg/7 lb (12–14 portions)	As loin

Oven Temperature	Special Points	Accompaniments
220 c, 425 f, gas 7 for 25 mins, then 190 c, 375 f, gas 5 for 25 mins per 500 g/1 lb	Pork must be well cooked	Apple and Cumberland sauce or crab-apple or cranberry jelly, roast or noisette potatoes, roasted apples. Stuffing or country herb dumplings
As leg	As leg	As leg Herb or apple and nut stuffing
As leg	Compact, inexpensive joint	As leg
As leg	Second quality. Inexpensive, rather fat	As leg
As leg	Second quality. Inexpensive, rather fat	As leg
220 c, 425 f, gas 7 for 20 mins, then 190 c, 375 f, gas 5 for 20 mins per 500 g/1 lb + 20 mins	Very lean meat. Baste frequently. Cook thoroughly	Country herb dumplings, roast potatoes
As leg + 5 mins per 500 g/1 lb	As above	Stuffing or herb dumplings, roast potatoes
As leg	As leg	As above

Meat Roasting

When catering for larger numbers a large roast has certain advantages because it is quick to prepare. However, it is not quick to cook; an average-sized whole leg of pork will take 5 hours to cook and you also need to allow some time for it to rest before carving it. A more practical solution may be to cook two half-sized joints. In the case of rib of beef, have it boned and rolled to facilitate carving. As bone conducts heat, when it is removed you will need to allow an extra 5 minutes' cooking time for each 500 g/1 lb of meat.

When you roast meat you must allow for shrinkage as well as wastage from bone weight. If you roast in a moderate oven (180 c, 350 f, gas 4), rather than a moderately hot oven (200 c, 400 f, gas 6), and cover the meat with foil, it will shrink less but take longer to cook.

Pan Gravy for Roasts

Remove cooked joints from roasting pan and leave to cool and set, ready for carving. Discard any bones browning in the pan. Allow sediment to settle, then carefully pour off fat without disturbing sediment. Add brown stock (see page 32) or liquor drained from accompanying vegetables. Reduce by boiling, scraping up the sediment in pan. Strain, skim off fat, adjust seasoning and reheat.

Serve in a warm sauceboat. Allow a minimum of 300 ml/$\frac{1}{2}$ pint of gravy for 6 servings.

Pot Roasting or Braising

This is the best method for roasting less tender meat. The large beef, veal and pork joints can be cut to desired weight.

Quality Guide

Allow 175–200 g/6–7 oz meat + 50 g/2 oz vegetables for each portion.

Suitable Joints

BEEF: Topside and leg of mutton cut. Aitchbone. Boned brisket and thick flank, boned and rolled.
PORK: Spare rib joint; lean belly, boned and rolled, with or without stuffing.
LAMB: Shoulder, breast, boned and rolled, with or without stuffing.
VEAL: Breast, shoulder, boned and rolled, with or without stuffing.

Method

Brown the joint all over quickly in hot dripping in a flameproof casserole. Add 100 g/4 oz onions and 125 g/4$\frac{1}{2}$ oz carrots to each 500 g/1 lb meat and brown lightly. Small pieces of pickled pork add flavour. Add a glass of wine and sufficient stock to come half-way up the joint. Season with salt and freshly ground black pepper, and add a bouquet garni with a celery stalk. Bring to the boil, cover and simmer gently, either on the stove or in a moderate oven (180 C, 350 F, gas 4) for 30 minutes per 500 g/1 lb.

Test with cooking fork and when tender remove joint and vegetables to warm serving dish. Skim fat from gravy with soft paper, adjust seasoning and reheat. Strain into heated sauce boat.

NOTE: *If no flameproof casserole is available, brown meat and vegetables in a frying pan with the wine, pour over the meat and add stock. Cover and continue cooking as above.*

POULTRY AND GAME

To save preparation time when buying poultry
for large numbers, and also to make it easier to
assess the quantity required, buy the bird already
dressed. If you are planning to make a casserole
dish get your butcher to cut the bird into joints.
This also saves time and is more economical than
buying chicken portions.

SERVING QUANTITIES

The weight of the bones varies according to the type of bird. Duck, and geese have heavy bones while chicken and turkey yield a higher proportion of meat to bone, so are more economical. You should allow the following weights per person:

chicken and game birds	275 g/10 oz
duck (domestic)	500 g/1 lb 1½ oz
goose	500 g/1 lb 1½ oz
turkey	300–350 g/11–13 oz

Chicken

Chickens vary in weight from baby poussins, weighing about 500 g/1 lb 2 oz each to capons and poulardes (neutered chickens and fowls) which weigh 2.25–3.5 kg/5–8 lb. The latter are expensive to rear and therefore cost more to buy. For 12 people it is, therefore, usually more economical to buy three chickens weighing 1.5–1.75 kg/3¼–4 lb each, which will divide easily into four portions each, rather than two capons, weighing 2.25 kg/5 lb each.

Young tender birds have white skin which should be unbroken and the end of the breastbone should be flexible gristle. This becomes rigid with maturity.

If you are buying frozen birds, allow 48 hours for defrosting, this also improves the flavour. Frozen birds are sold without giblets.

CHICKEN WITH A CHEESE AND WINE SAUCE

This delightful Alpine recipe is a good choice for a party as most of the preparation can be done in advance and the dish can be finished in the oven just before serving.

No. of servings	6	12	24	48
chicken (about 2 kg/4½ lb each)	1	2	4	8
vegetables and herbs for stock (page 32)				
butter	75 g/3 oz	150 g/5½ oz	300 g/11 oz	600 g/1¼ lb
tarragon, chopped fresh	2 tablespoons	4 tablespoons	8 tablespoons	16 tablespoons
dried	1 tablespoon	2 tablespoons	3 tablespoons	6 tablespoons
salt and freshly ground black pepper	to taste	to taste	to taste	to taste

SAUCE

butter	50 g/2 oz	100 g/4 oz	200 g/7 oz	400 g/14 oz
flour	50 g/2 oz	100 g/4 oz	200 g/7 oz	400 g/14 oz
giblet stock	150 ml/¼ pint	300 ml/½ pint	600 ml/1 pint	1.2 litres/2 pints
dry white wine	150 ml/¼ pint	300 ml/½ pint	600 ml/1 pint	1.2 litres/2 pints
Gruyère or Emmental cheese, grated	60 g/2 oz	120 g/4 oz	240 g/8 oz	480 g/1 lb
single cream	300 ml/½ pint	600 ml/1 pint	1.2 litres/2 pints	2.4 litres/4 pints
French mustard	2 teaspoons	4 teaspoons	3 tablespoons	6 tablespoons
salt and pepper	to taste	to taste	to taste	to taste

TOPPING

dried breadcrumbs	60 g/2 oz	120 g/4 oz	240 g/8 oz	480 g/1 lb
Cheddar cheese, grated	60 g/2 oz	120 g/4 oz	240 g/8 oz	480 g/1 lb

GARNISH *fresh tarragon or parsley*

Set the oven at moderately hot (200 C, 400 F, gas 6).

Clean the giblets, cover with water, add the herbs, seasoning and suitable vegetables to make a stock (see page 32) and leave to simmer.

Cream the butter and tarragon, season well and spread over the chicken. Place in the heated oven and roast for 1 hour or until tender. Turn and baste the bird from time to time.

For the sauce: melt the butter and, off the heat, add the flour to make a roux. Gradually blend in the strained giblet stock. Bring to a simmer and slowly add the wine and continue cooking gently for 5 minutes. Stir in the grated cheese and the cream. Do not allow the sauce to boil again. Season with mustard, salt and pepper. Cover and keep warm in a bain-marie.

When cooked, take the bird out of the roasting tin and reserve the pan juices. Divide the chickens into 6 portions; separate the thighs and drumsticks and halve the breasts. Generously butter a warmed gratin dish and arrange the chicken pieces in a single layer; coat them evenly with the sauce.

For the topping; mix the dried breadcrumbs with the grated cheese and sprinkle this over the sauce. Trickle over the remaining tarragon butter from the roasting pan.

The dish can now be set aside and finished off when required. To serve straightaway; set the oven at hot (220 C, 425 F, gas 7) and place the gratin dish in it for 10–15 minutes until the crust is bubbling and golden.

If the dish is being heated from cold, place it in a moderately hot oven (200 C, 400 F, gas 6) for 10 minutes or so longer to ensure it is heated through.

Serve garnished with fresh tarragon or parsley.

Accompany with sauté potatoes or buttered noodles and peas or green beans.

COQ AU VIN

ILLUSTRATED ON PAGES 166–7

In this famous Burgundian dish the bird is jointed but it may also be casseroled whole. If pickled pork is used, less salt will be required in the sauce than if fried bacon is substituted.

No. of servings	6	12	24	48
chicken (about 2 kg/4½ lb each)	1	2	4	8
unsalted butter	75 g/3 oz	150 g/5½ oz	300 g/11 oz	600 g/1¼ lb
pickled pork, or bacon cut into lardon	100 g/4 oz	200 g/7 oz	400 g/14 oz	800 g/1¾ lb
button onions	225 g/8 oz	450 g/1 lb	900 g/2 lb	1.8 kg/4 lb
garlic clove, crushed	1	2	4	8
button mushrooms	75 g/3 oz	150 g/5½ oz	300 g/11 oz	600 g/1¼ lb
brandy	2 tablespoons	4 tablespoons	120 ml/4 fl oz	240 ml/7½ fl oz
Burgundy or dry red	300 ml/½ pint	600 ml/1 pint	1.2 litres/2 pints	2.4 litres/4 pints
bouquet garni	1	1	2	3
salt and pepper	to taste	to taste	to taste	to taste
stock (page 32)	600 ml/1 pint	1.2 litres/2 pints	2 litres/3½ pints	3.5 litres/6 pints
BEURRE MANIÉ				
butter	50 g/2 oz	100 g/4 oz	200 g/7 oz	400 g/14 oz
flour	50 g/2 oz	100 g/4 oz	200 g/7 oz	400 g/14 oz

GARNISH *glazed button onions; fried triangles of bread and chopped parsley*

Set the oven at moderate (170 c, 325 f, gas 3).

Joint the chicken into 6 portions. Heat the butter with the pickled pork or bacon and cook gently until the fat runs. Add the onions, garlic and mushrooms and fry lightly. Add the chicken joints and fry until golden. Warm the brandy, ignite it and pour it over the chicken. When the flames die down, add the wine and the bouquet garni. Stir in enough stock to just cover the chicken and season.

Bring to the simmer, cover and cook gently on top of the stove or place in the heated oven for 1 hour or until tender. Remove the chicken joints to a heated earthenware serving dish and keep warm.

Cream the butter and flour together to make the beurre manié. Divide into small pieces and add to the sauce, stirring over a gentle heat until it reaches the right consistency. Adjust the seasoning and pour over the chicken.

To make the garnish: fry triangles of bread, dip the corners in chopped parsley and arrange them round the edge of the dish. Then put the glazed button onions in the centre on top of the chicken. Serve with creamed or new potatoes and buttered spinach.

CHICKEN WITH LEMON SAUCE

ILLUSTRATED ON PAGE 48

This is easy to prepare and with its delicate lemon and artichoke flavour makes a refreshing summer meal. Canned artichoke bases are readily available and should not be confused with canned baby artichoke hearts.

No. of servings	6	12	24	48
chickens, (about 2 kg/4½ lb each)	1	2	4	8
flour, for coating				
butter	40 g/1½ oz	80 g/3 oz	160 g/6 oz	320 g/11½ oz
onion, chopped	50 g/2 oz	100 g/4 oz	200 g/7 oz	400 g/14 oz
dry white wine	200 ml/7 fl oz	400 ml/14 fl oz	800 ml/1¼ pints	1.6 litres/2½ pints
canned artichoke bases	300 g/11 oz	600 g/1¼ lb	1.2 kg/2½ lb	2.4 kg/5½ lb
chicken stock, about	1 litre/1¾ pints	2 litres/3½ pints	4 litres/7 pints	8 litres/14 pints
small lemons, zest	2	4	8	12
double cream	150 ml/¼ pint	300 ml/½ pint	600 ml/1 pint	1.2 litres/2¼ pints
salt and pepper	to taste	to taste	to taste	to taste

GARNISH *lemon and orange slices*

Divide the chicken into 6 joints: breasts, thighs and drumsticks.

Coat the chicken joints with flour, patting off the surplus. Heat the butter and fry the onion in it until softened. Add the chicken joints and fry them golden brown on both sides. Pour in the wine and bubble for a few minutes. Add the liquid from the artichoke can and enough stock to cover the chicken. Grate the zest off the lemons into the pan. Cover and simmer very gently for 40 minutes or until the legs are tender. Add the artichoke bases half way through the cooking time.

Remove the artichokes and the chicken to a warmed serving dish, separating the thighs and drumsticks and halving the breast portions.

Reduce the sauce slightly by boiling it rapidly. Blend some of the sauce with the cream and stir it into the pan. Heat through, seasoning to taste, and pour it over the chicken. Garnish with lemon and orange slices.

CHICKEN PAPRIKA

ILLUSTRATED ON PAGE 76

This version of the famous Hungarian dish with its rosy sauce, can be made in advance and reheated, it also freezes very successfully.

No. of servings	6	12	24	48
chicken (about 2 kg/4½ lb each)	1	2	4	8
flour, for coating				
butter or margarine	75 g/3 oz	150 g/5½ oz	300 g/11 oz	600 g/1¼ lb
onion, chopped	150 g/6 oz	300 g/11 oz	600 g/1¼ lb	1.2 kg/2½ lb
mushrooms, sliced	150 g/6 oz	300 g/11 oz	600 g/1¼ lb	1.2 kg/2½ lb
flour, about	65 g/2½ oz	130 g/4½ oz	260 g/1¼ lb	500 g/1 lb 2 oz
chicken stock, about (page 32)	600 ml/1 pint	1.2 litres/2 pints	2.4 litres/4 pints	4.8 litres/8 pints
milk	300 ml/½ pint	600 ml/1 pint	1.2 litres/2 pints	2.4 litres/4 pints
salt and pepper	to taste	to taste	to taste	to taste
tomato purée	75 g/3 oz	150 g/5 oz	300 g/11 oz	600 g/1¼ lb
paprika	3 teaspoons	1½ tablespoons	3 tablespoons	6 tablespoons
sugar	to taste	to taste	to taste	to taste
single cream	200 ml/7 fl oz	400 ml/14 fl oz	800 ml/1¼ pints	1.6 litres/2¾ pints

GARNISH *mushroom slices, fried; paprika, to decorate*

Joint each chicken into 6 portions.

Flour chicken joints. Heat fat and fry joints until golden, turning once. Remove from pan. Fry onions and mushrooms in hot fat until softened. Stir in enough flour to absorb the fat. Gradually blend in chicken stock and milk, season. Bring to a simmer, stirring, and cook for 5 minutes. Blend together tomato purée, paprika, sugar and cream.

Mix in some of the sauce, gradually stir this into pan. Add the chicken joints and enough extra stock to ensure that the sauce covers the chicken. Cover and simmer gently for 30–40 minutes until tender. Stir occasionally to prevent sticking. Do not allow to boil or the sauce will separate.

Present in a border of fluffy rice, garnished with fried mushroom slices, and sprinkled with paprika.

APRICOT AND HONEY BARBECUED CHICKEN

ILLUSTRATED ON PAGE 85

These chicken joints can either be barbecued or they can be baked in a hot oven.
Good accompaniments are grilled corn on the cob and jacket potatoes.

No. of servings	6	12	24	48
chicken joints	6	12	24	48
chicken seasoning or paprika	to taste	to taste	to taste	to taste
SAUCE				
canned apricot halves	400 g/14 oz	800 g/1¾ lb	1.6 kg/3½ lb	3.2 kg/7 lb
soya sauce	1½ tablespoons	3 tablespoons	90 ml/4 fl oz	180 ml/6 fl oz
honey	1½ tablespoons	3 tablespoons	90 ml/4 fl oz	180 ml/6 fl oz
tomato ketchup	1½ tablespoons	3 tablespoons	90 ml/4 fl oz	180 ml/6 fl oz
dried rosemary	¼ teaspoon	½ teaspoon	1 teaspoon	2 teaspoons
lemon juice	1½ tablespoons	3 tablespoons	90 ml/4 fl oz	180 ml/6 fl oz
salt and pepper	to taste	to taste	to taste	to taste
chicken stock	300 ml/½ pint	600 ml/1 pint	1.2 litres/2 pints	2.4 litres/ 4 pints

Set the oven at hot (200 c, 400 f, gas 6), if used.

Brush the chicken joints with oil and season with chicken seasoning or paprika to give it a rosy colour. Put the joints on a barbecue grid or in an oiled roasting dish, if you are going to bake them in the oven.

Strain the juices off the apricots and purée the fruit in a blender. Heat gently with the soya sauce, honey, tomato ketchup, rosemary and lemon juice, stirring well. If you are baking the joints in the oven, spoon the sauce over the joints, place them in the heated oven and bake for 30 minutes or until tender. Turn and baste with the sauce halfway through the cooking time. Remove the chicken joints to a warmed serving dish. Add the stock to the roasting tin and boil up, adjust the seasoning as necessary and pour over the joints.

If you are barbecuing the joints add the chicken stock to the apricot mixture, reduce it until thickened and adjust the seasoning. Brush the joints with this sauce as required and cook until tender. Serve with the remaining sauce.

Grilled Corn on the Cob

Choose young corn with fresh green husks. Peel back the husks and remove the silk. Spread the corn with butter and cover again with the husks. Grill on a barbecue or on a grill until tender, turning frequently. Remove the husks and spread with well seasoned butter when serving.

CHICKEN VÉRONIQUE

ILLUSTRATED ON PAGE 18

This is a very practical dish which can be prepared in advance. It is perfect for a fork lunch or supper and is a good choice for a wedding buffet.

No. of servings	6	12	24	48
chickens (about 2 kg/4½ lb each)	1	2	4	8
stock				
tarragon, chopped fresh	2 teaspoons	1 tablespoon	2 tablespoons	3 tablespoons
dried	1 teaspoon	2 teaspoons	1 tablespoon	1½ tablespoons
SAUCE				
egg yolks	3	6	12	24
single cream	150 ml/¼ pint	300 ml/½ pint	600 ml/1 pint	1.2 litres/2 pints
dry white wine	100 ml/3½ fl oz	200 ml/7 fl oz	400 ml/14 fl oz	800 ml/1¼ pints
reduced chicken stock (see below)	300 ml/½ pint	600 ml/1 pint	1.2 litres/2 pints	2.4 litres/4 pints
lemon juice	3 teaspoons	1½–2 tablespoons	3–4 tablespoons	6–7 tablespoons
salt and pepper	to taste	to taste	to taste	to taste
white grapes, seedless (if available)	250 g/9 oz	350 g/12 oz	700 g/1½ lb	1.4 kg/3 lb

Divide the chicken into 6 joints. Cover the joints and the giblets with cold water, add the vegetables, herbs and seasoning, see chicken stock page 32. Bring quickly to the boil and simmer until the joints are tender. Remove joints and leave giblets cooking to make stock.

Skin the joints, remove the flesh from the bones and cut them into neat pieces. Strain the stock, return it to the saucepan, add the tarragon and cook uncovered until reduced by half.

To make the sauce: beat the yolks and cream together in a bowl and add the wine and the cooked reduced stock. Cook gently over a pan of simmering water or in a bain-marie until thickened to a creamy consistency which will coat the back of a wooden spoon. Remove the sauce from the heat and season to taste with salt, pepper and lemon juice. Slit and seed the grapes if they are not seedless. Add half of them to the sauce. Arrange the chicken pieces on shallow serving dishes and pour the sauce over it. Arrange the remaining grapes in an attractive pattern on top. Refrigerate until required. The sauce will thicken as it chills.

Serve with a green salad or minted potato salad made from new potatoes.

ORCHARD CHICKEN

The orchard fruits add colour to this chicken casserole and the stem ginger and spices give it an intriguing flavour.

No. of servings	6	12	24	48
chicken (2 kg/4½ lb each)	1	2	4	8
bay leaf	1	2	3	6
parsley sprig	1	2	4	8
salt and pepper	to taste	to taste	to taste	to taste
plums or apricots	225 g/½ lb	450 g/1 lb	900 g/2 lb	1.8 kg/4 lb
dessert apples	225 g/½ lb	450 g/1 lb	900 g/2 lb	1.8 kg/4 lb
pears	225 g/½ lb	450 g/1 lb	900 g/2 lb	1.8 kg/4 lb
vegetable oil	3 tablespoons	6 tablespoons	170 ml/6 fl oz	340 ml/12 fl oz
flour, for coating				
onion, chopped	150 g/6 oz	350 g/12 oz	675 g/1½ lb	1.3 kg/3 lb
coriander seed, crushed	1 teaspoon	2 teaspoons	4 teaspoons	2 tablespoons
cinnamon, ground	¼ teaspoon	½ teaspoon	1 teaspoon	2 teaspoons
saffron, powdered	¼ teaspoon	½ teaspoon	1 teaspoon	2 teaspoons
stem ginger knobs	3	6	150 g/6 oz	300 g/11 oz
ginger syrup	2 tablespoons	4 tablespoons	150 ml/¼ pint	300 ml/½ pint
lemon juice	to taste	to taste	to taste	to taste

GARNISH *minced fresh parsley*

Joint the chicken into 6 and remove the wing pinions. Skin the joints. Put the carcase and pinions with the herbs and seasoning in a pan and cover with water. Simmer to make a stock.

Halve and stone the plums or apricots, slice and core the apples and pears. Heat the fat in a flame-proof casserole or pan. Flour the chicken joints and fry them in the hot fat until crisp and golden. Remove from the pan and add the onion and fry until just beginning to colour. Replace the chicken and add enough stock to cover the joints. Mix in the coriander, cinnamon, saffron and chopped ginger knobs. Simmer for 20 minutes, then add the fruit and ginger syrup. Cover and simmer gently until the chicken is tender. Add lemon juice and seasoning to taste.

Serve, garnished, with minted, boiled potatoes or baked jacket potatoes.

DUCK WITH BIGARADE SAUCE

ILLUSTRATED ON PAGE 116

This delicious orange-flavoured sauce is particularly good with duck, both domesticated and wild. It is convenient for large parties as the duck can be roasted and carved in the kitchen and heated through and served in the sauce.

No. of servings	6	12	24	48
duck (about 2.5 kg/5½ lb each)	1	2	4	8
orange	1	2	4	8
BIGARADE SAUCE				
Espagnole Sauce (page 185)	300 ml/½ pint	600 ml/1 pint	1.2 litres/2 pints	2.4 litres/4 pints
orange, large	1	2	4	8
lemon, small	1	2	4	8
redcurrant jelly	2 tablespoons	4 tablespoons	8 tablespoons	16 tablespoons
port	30 ml/1 fl oz	60 ml/2 fl oz	120 ml/4 fl oz	240 ml/8 fl oz
butter, for frying				
duck liver	1	2	4	8
seasoning	to taste	to taste	to taste	to taste

GARNISH *orange twists; watercress sprigs*

Set the oven at moderately hot (200 c, 400 f, gas 6). Stuff the duck with a peeled orange and roast for 1½ hours or until just tender. Meanwhile, clean the giblets, set aside the liver and make giblet stock (see page 32).

When the duck is ready, lift it out of the roasting tin, allowing the juices to flow back into the tin. Set it aside for carving. Carefully pour off the surplus fat from the tin and add about 150 ml/¼ pint of giblet stock for each duck. Boil briskly and reduce, scraping up the residue from the pan. Add this to the Espagnole sauce. Grate the rind off the orange and lemon, avoiding the pith and add it to the sauce with the juice, redcurrant jelly and port. Chop the duck liver and fry it gently. Add it to the sauce. Cook the sauce gently until the jelly is melted and adjust the seasoning.

Carve the duck into portions, arrange it on a warmed serving dish, pour over the sauce and heat through. Garnish with orange twists and watercress sprigs.

Serve with Duchess potatoes or potato purée, with celeriac and swedes (see page 136) and green beans or Brussels sprouts.

*Game pie (see page 122); Brussels Sprouts with
Chestnuts (see page 135) and creamed potatoes*

*Scallops Coquilles St. Jacques (see page 54); Duck with
Bigarade Sauce (see page 114) and Hasselback Potatoes
(see page 139)*

116

GUINEA CHICK WITH MUSHROOM, CREAM AND BRANDY SAUCE

Guinea chicks, if cut in half, are the right size for this dish. Alternatively, you could use partridge, allowing one for each person (this is more expensive). Chicken or turkey breasts weighing 100–150g/4–5oz are less expensive and are also good.

No. of servings	6	12	24	48
guinea chicks	3	6	12	24
stock, game or chicken	500 ml/17 fl oz	1 litre/1¾ pints	2 litres/3½ pints	4 litres/7 pints
butter	75 g/3 oz	150 g/5½ oz	300 g/11 oz	600 g/1½ lb
onion, chopped	50 g/2 oz	100 g/4 oz	200 g/7 oz	400 g/14 oz
brandy, about	100 ml/3½ fl oz	200 ml/7 fl oz	400 ml/14 fl oz	800 ml/1¼ pints
ground nutmeg	¼ teaspoon	½ teaspoon	1 teaspoon	2 teaspoons
dried rosemary	½ teaspoon	1 teaspoon	2 teaspoons	4 teaspoons
button mushrooms	150 g/5½ oz	300 g/11 oz	600 g/1½ lb	1.2 kg/3 lb
BEURRE MANIÉ				
flour	50 g/2 oz	100 g/4 oz	200 g/7 oz	400 g/14 oz
butter	50 g/2 oz	100 g/4 oz	200 g/7 oz	400 g/14 oz
single cream	150 ml/¼ pint	300 ml/½ pint	600 ml/1 pint	1.2 litres/2 pints
salt and pepper	to taste	to taste	to taste	to taste

GARNISH *fresh rosemary sprigs or parsley*

Cut the guinea chicks in half. Clean and put the giblets into the stock, cover and simmer gently.

Heat the butter and fry the onion gently in it until softened. Turn up the heat, put the guinea chick halves in and brown quickly. Warm half the brandy, and pour over the birds and flame. Shake until the flames are out. Add stock, nutmeg and dried rosemary. Cover and simmer gently on top of the stove for 30 minutes. Add mushrooms and continue cooking for 30 minutes or until tender. Remove to a serving dish, keep warm.

For the beurre manié: cream together the flour and butter, divide it into small pieces and gradually whisk it into the sauce over a low heat and simmer until the sauce thickens. Mix together the remaining brandy, cream and a little sauce and blend this into the sauce in the pan. Adjust the seasoning, heat through, and pour over the guinea chicks.

Garnish with sprigs of rosemary or parsley then serve with buttered potatoes, leaf spinach or mange tout peas.

GAME

There are two kinds of game: feathered and furred and both of them have lean meat. If you like your game highly flavoured then it should be hung for a longer time than if a less gamey flavour is preferred. Always hang game in a cool, airy place. Wild duck, unlike the domestic variety, is not fatty. So that game birds do not dry out when they are cooking they have to be trussed with a thin slice of pork fat over the breast, this is called larding. Hare and venison should be marinated in wine and oil and flavoured with herbs and vegetables (see page 130) before cooking.

Game	Season	No. of servings, about	Cooking time in a moderately hot (200 C, 400 F, gas 6) oven
grouse	mid Aug–mid Dec	1–2	30 minutes
partridge	Sept–Feb	1–2	30 minutes
pheasant	Oct–Feb	3–4	45–50 minutes
quail	all year	1	15 minutes
wild duck	Sept–Feb best Nov and Dec	2	30–45 minutes
wood pigeon	all year but best March–Oct	1–2	60 minutes, about
hare (saddle or baron)	Aug–end Feb	4–6	40–45 minutes, about
venison, saddle or haunch	late June–Jan	250–300 g/8–11 oz per portion	15–20 minutes

Roasting Game Birds

Only young game birds can be roasted. They have clean pliable feet, older birds have horney feet and scaly legs and need slow casserole cooking. Frozen birds can be roasted, but are usually better casseroled in a tasty sauce. You can adapt many chicken dishes for pheasant.

Partridge and pheasants are roasted in the same way as chicken, in other words, in a moderately hot oven (200 C, 400 F, gas 6). Grouse is roasted in a hot oven (220 C, 425 F, gas 7) and for all these birds the gravy is made in the same way as for chicken. The flavour will be improved if the roasting tin is deglazed with wine before the giblet stock is added.

When you serve the game birds, remove the trussing string and the barding fat. Place the small birds on hot fried croûtons the same size as the bird. Replace the tail feathers of pheasants as decoration.

Garnish with a sprig of watercress, game chips and breadcrumbs fried golden brown in butter. Serve with gravy and bread sauce. Chestnut and potato purée (see page 136) is a good accompaniment.

Roasting Hare

Only a leveret (young hare) is suitable for roasting. The saddle (back) will yield 4 portions, the baron (back with the hind legs attached) 6 portions. The rest can be used for casseroles, game pie or pâté. A mature male hare is suitable for jugging and a large one will yield 8 portions.

To roast a hare: remove the thin skin from the saddle, lard with strips of pork fat and marinate overnight. Alternatively, marinate and then cover with thin rashers of streaky bacon.

Set the oven at hot (220 c, 425 f, gas 7).

Generously butter a roasting tin. Secure the bacon covering with string and put in the roasting tin. Place in the heated oven and bake for 40 minutes or until tender, basting frequently.

Remove to a serving dish and pour off the fat from the roasting tin. Deglaze the pan with a glass of sherry or port and an equal quantity of stock, boil up, scraping up the residue from the tin. Stir in 120 ml/4 fl oz of double or soured cream, heat through and season to taste.

Before serving, remove the string and bacon, and carve the saddle lengthwise down either side of the backbone into slices. Arrange these on the serving plate and pour over the sauce. Garnish with the crispy bacon, stuffing balls and parsley or watercress.

Serve with redcurrant or cranberry jelly, straw potatoes and red cabbage.

Roast Haunch of Venison

This is a good joint when catering for 12 or more, but it must be well hung and marinated to be tender. It is very lean and needs protecting during roasting or it will dry. Until the advent of foil, it was encased in huff paste, a flour and water crust, but foil is easier to use.

Haunch varies in weight according to the type of deer – red, roebuck or fallow. A joint weighing 3 kg/6½ lb will yield 12 good portions. In Scotland a red wine marinade is used, while in the West Country cider is customary.

Place the venison in the marinade (see page 130) and leave for 24 hours, or 48 hours if a more gamey flavour is preferred, turning from time to time.

Set the oven at hot (220 c, 425 f, gas 7).

Place in a generously buttered roasting tin, strain over the marinade and cover the tin with buttered foil. Put in the heated oven and bake for 20 minutes. Lift the foil, baste with the marinade and cover again. Reduce the heat to moderate (180 c, 350 f, gas 4) and continue cooking, allowing 20 minutes for each 500 g/1 lb 2 oz, basting frequently. Remove the foil for the last 15 minutes of cooking, dredge the haunch with flour and pour melted butter over it. When nicely browned, place the venison on a serving dish. Carefully pour off any surplus fat from the roasting tin and add stock, preferably game, scraping up the residue from the tin and adjust the seasoning. Strain into a warm gravy boat.

Serve the venison with gravy and rowan or cranberry jelly, celeriac or chestnut and potato purée (see page 136). Red or green cabbage also make a good accompaniment.

Venison saddle and best end of neck can also be roasted in this way.

Rabbit

Domesticated rabbits bred for eating are plump with white flesh and are excellent for sautéing or making into a blanquette. Wild rabbit is smaller, has a slightly gamey flavour and makes tasty casseroles and stews.

Rabbit is usually sold by weight, already jointed. Allow 200–250 g/7–8¾ oz per portion. The joints should be soaked for 2 hours in cold salted water and wiped dry before cooking.

VENISON CUTLETS WITH ROB ROY SAUCE

Cutlets from young, but well hung deer are best for this dish. The whisky and juniper berry sauce gives the game an excellent flavour. Marinate the venison for 24–48 hours before cooking to tenderize and flavour it.

No. of servings	6	12	24	48
venison neck cutlets	6	12	24	48
lemon, juice	1	1½	2	3
juniper berries, crushed	1 tablespoon	2 tablespoons	4 tablespoons	8 tablespoons
fresh thyme or marjoram	1 teaspoon	2 teaspoons	4 teaspoons	3 tablespoons
salt and pepper	to taste	to taste	to taste	to taste
MARINADE:				
cider vinegar	4 tablespoons	175 ml/6 fl oz	350 ml/12 fl oz	700 ml/24 fl oz
whisky	4 tablespoons	175 ml/6 fl oz	350 ml/12 fl oz	700 ml/24 fl oz
vegetable oil	120 ml/4 fl oz	220 ml/8 fl oz	450 ml/16 fl oz	900 ml/1½ pints
carrots, sliced	50 g/2 oz	100 g/4 oz	225 g/8 oz	450 g/1 lb
onion, sliced	75 g/3 oz	275 g/6 oz	350 g/12 oz	700 g/1½ lb
bay leaf	1	1	2	3
SAUCE:				
streaky bacon	50 g/2 oz	100 g/4 oz	225 g/8 oz	450 g/1 lb
butter	25 g/1 oz	50 g/2 oz	100 g/4 oz	225 g/8 oz
celery, chopped	50 g/2 oz	100 g/4 oz	225 g/8 oz	450 g/1 lb
flour	25 g/1 oz	50 g/2 oz	100 g/4 oz	225 g/8 oz
stock, about	300 ml/½ pint	600 ml/1 pint	1.2 ml/2 pints	2.4 ml/4 pints
small orange, juice of	1	2	4	8
cranberry sauce	2 tablespoons	4 tablespoons	100 g/4 oz	225 g/8 oz

GARNISH *croûtons; celery leaves*

Trim the venison cutlets and rub with lemon juice. Mix together juniper berries and herbs and rub into the cutlets. Season with salt and black pepper.

Make the marinade: mix the vinegar, whisky and oil together and pour over the cutlets. Add the carrots, onion and bay leaf. Marinate the meat for

24–48 hours, turning occasionally. Prior to cooking drain the cutlets and dry them well on kitchen paper. Remove the rind and gristle from the bacon and chop it up. Cook slowly until crisp and fat runs. Add butter to the pan, heat and seal the cutlets in it. Remove the meat from the pan. Fry the celery. Stir in the flour and fry, stirring until brown. Remove pan from heat and stir in stock and strained marinade. Bring to simmer and cook until thickened. Replace cutlets and add extra stock if required, to cover meat. Adjust seasoning.

Cover and simmer on top of stove or in moderate oven for 1½ hours or until tender. Stir in orange juice and cranberry sauce and season to taste.

Dress the cutlets standing up round a mound of Chestnut and potato purée (see page 136). Garnish in between the cutlets with croûtons cut into diamond or crescent shapes and fried crisp and golden. Arrange tufts of fresh celery leaves around the base.

Hand the sauce separately and serve with buttered Brussels sprouts, cabbage or broccoli.

MUSTARD RABBIT

In the French version of this dish white wine and cream are used instead of cider.

No. of servings	6	12	24	48
rabbit joints	1.4 kg/3¼ lb	2.7 kg/6 lb	5.4 kg/12 lb	10.8 kg/24 lb
made mustard, for coating				
flour, for coating				
green streaky bacon	50 g/2 oz	100 g/4 oz	200 g/7 oz	400 g/14 oz
unsalted butter	50 g/2 oz	100 g/4 oz	200 g/7 oz	400 g/14 oz
onion, finely chopped	100 g/4 oz	200 g/7 oz	400 g/14 oz	800 g/1¾ lb
dry white wine or cider	100 ml/3½ fl oz	200 ml/7 fl oz	400 ml/14 fl oz	800 ml/1¼ pints
stock, game or white, about	100 ml/3½ fl oz	200 ml/7 fl oz	400 ml/14 fl oz	800 ml/1¼ pints

GARNISH *fried triangles of bread; chopped chervil or parsley*

Soak the rabbit for 2 hours in cold, salted water and wipe dry. Spread each joint with mustard and leave in a cold place overnight. Set the oven at moderate (160 C, 325 F, gas 3). Next day, dredge lightly with flour and shake off the surplus. Take the rind off the bacon rashers and chop up. Heat the fat in a flameproof casserole or sauté pan and fry the rabbit joints until nicely brown on both sides. Remove from the pan and fry the bacon and onion gently until softened. Replace the rabbit, add wine or cider. Bring to a simmer, cover and

continue cooking, stirring occasionally, on top of the stove or place in the oven for 30 minutes. Add cream and more stock, if required, bring to a simmer and adjust seasoning. Cover and continue cooking, stirring occasionally, for 45 minutes until the rabbit is tender.

Serve garnished with triangles of fried bread and chopped chervil or parsley. Accompany with boiled or château potatoes, and broccoli or Brussels sprouts.

GAME PIE

ILLUSTRATED ON PAGE 115

This is an extremely flexible dish and you can vary the game you use according to what you have to hand. Partridge or pheasant can be used very successfully instead of grouse and mature birds are ideal for pies and pâtés.
The pie can be made in advance and either reheated, or served cold if you make it with puff pastry.

No. of servings	6	12	24	48
mature grouse or wood pigeon	2	4	8	16
butter, softened for spreading over birds				
hare, jointed or	½	1	2	4
venison shoulder	75 g/3 oz	150 g/5 oz	300 g/11 oz	600 g/1¼ lb
pickled belly of pork, or bacon hock	250 g/9 oz	500 g/1 lb 2 oz	1 kg/2¼ lb	2 kg/4½ lb
onion, sliced	100 g/4 oz	250 g/9 oz	400 g/14 oz	800 g/1¾ lb
butter	40 g/1½ oz	75 g/3 oz	150 g/5 oz	300 g/11 oz
celery, cleaned	50 g/2 oz	75 g/3 oz	150 g/5 oz	300 g/11 oz
carrots, cleaned	50 g/2 oz	100 g/4 oz	200 g/7 oz	400 g/14 oz
bouquet garni (parsley, bayleaf, thyme)	1	1	2	4
salt and freshly ground pepper	to taste	to taste	to taste	to taste
savory, chopped fresh	2 teaspoons	1 tablespoon	2 tablespoons	4 tablespoons
dried	1 teaspoon	2 teaspoons	1 tablespoon	2 tablespoons
lemon rind, grated	1 teaspoon	2 teaspoons	1 tablespoon	2 tablespoons
mushrooms, sliced	100 g/4 oz	200 g/7 oz	400 g/14 oz	800 g/1¾ lb
port or sherry or	50 ml/2 fl oz	100 ml/3½ fl oz	200 ml/7 fl oz	400 ml/14 fl oz
cider	100 ml/3½ fl oz	200 ml/7 fl oz	400 ml/14 fl oz	800 ml/1¾ pints
parsley, finely chopped	1 tablespoon	2 tablespoons	4 tablespoons	6 tablespoons

flaky or puff pastry	250 g/9 oz	500 g/1 lb 2 oz	1 kg/2¼ lb	2 kg/4½ lb

egg, for glazing

GARNISH *parsley sprigs*

Set the oven at hot (220 c, 425 f, gas 7).

Truss the birds, spread them with butter and roast them for 15–20 minutes until browned. Remove from the oven, fillet off the breasts and set aside.

Remove the rind on the pork or bacon and cut into chunks. If using venison, slice thickly and cut into pieces. Melt the butter and fry the onion with the pork or bacon in it until softened. Add the hare joints or venison meat and brown. Put the carcass of the birds, giblets and hare liver in a large pan with the hare or venison, fried pork or bacon and onion. Add the celery sticks and carrots in large pieces. Cover with water and add the herbs and seasoning. Bring to the boil, skim and simmer slowly for 2 hours until the meat is tender.

Strain off the stock through a coarse sieve. Remove the flesh from the carcasses of the birds and mince with the pork or bacon and hare liver. Mix in the savory and grated lemon rind and season with salt and freshly ground pepper.

Put a pie funnel in the centre of the pie dish and spread the minced meat over the base. Slice the breasts of the birds. Remove the flesh from the hare joints and slice. Fill the pie with layers of well mixed game and sliced mushrooms. Moisten each layer with port or cider and sprinkle with parsley and seasoning.

Skim the fat off the stock by passing kitchen paper across it. Adjust the seasoning. Pour enough over the pie filling to three-quarters fill the dish.

Roll out the pastry and cover the pie. Decorate with leaves and a tassel cut from the trimmings. Make 4 slits for the steam to escape and glaze with egg wash. Place in the heated oven and bake for 20 minutes until well risen. Reduce the heat to (190 c, 375 f, gas 5) for a further 20 minutes until golden and cooked through. You can either serve this dish hot with spiced red cabbage and stuffed baked potatoes. Alternatively, you can serve it cold with a red cabbage and apple salad and a mixed winter salad.

SALMIS OF GAME

This is a rich game stew made with maturer game birds or hare, or the less tender cuts of venison. Allow 175 g/6 oz of boneless game meat for each person. It is enriched with port, madeira, whisky or red wine and flavoured with juniper berries and herbs.

No. of servings	6	12	24	48
game meat, boneless	1 kg/2¼ lb	2 kg/4½ lb	4 kg/9 lb	8 kg/18 lb
flour	75 g/3 oz	150 g/5 oz	300 g/11 oz	600 g/1¼ lb
bacon, chopped	100 g/4 oz	200 g/7 oz	400 g/14 oz	800 g/1¾ lb
butter or dripping	50 g/2 oz	100 g/4 oz	200 g/7 oz	400 g/14 oz
onion, chopped	100 g/4 oz	200 g/7 oz	400 g/14 oz	800 g/1¾ lb
celery, chopped	50 g/2 oz	100 g/4 oz	200 g/7 oz	400 g/14 oz
carrots, chopped	50 g/2 oz	100 g/4 oz	200 g/7 oz	400 g/14 oz
red wine, whisky or port or madeira	75 ml/3 fl oz	150 ml/¼ pint	300 ml/½ pint	600 ml/1 pint
game stock, about	1 litre/1¾ pints	2 litres/3½ pints	4 litres/7 pints	8 litres/14 pints
juniper berries	1 teaspoon	2 teaspoons	1 tablespoon	2 tablespoons
mixed herbs	½ teaspoon	1 teaspoon	2 teaspoons	4 teaspoons
salt and black pepper	to taste	to taste	to taste	to taste
lemon juice	to taste	to taste	to taste	to taste

GARNISH *chopped fresh parsley; fried croûtons*

Set the oven at moderate (160 C, 325 F, gas 3).

Cut the meat into neat pieces, toss them in flour and shake off the surplus. Fry the chopped bacon slowly until the fat runs. Add the butter and fry the onion and celery until softened. Put in the carrots and meat and continue frying until nicely coloured. Stir in enough flour to absorb the fat, and brown. Add the wine or whisky, bubble for a minute or two and pour in enough stock to cover.

Crush and add the juniper berries, herbs and seasoning. Bring to a simmer and cook gently on top of the stove for 2 hours or place in the heated oven for 2 hours or until the meat is tender. Adjust the seasoning and sharpen with lemon juice. Add more stock if required.

Serve garnished with chopped fresh parsley and triangles of fried bread. Accompany with a purée of potatoes and celeriac or swedes.

ABOVE: *Bisque of Shellfish (see page 49) and Lamb Cutlets in Pastry (see page 99)*
OVERLEAF: *Lombardy Terrine (see page 27); Turbot Dugléré (see page 62); Italian-style Haricots Verts (see page 134); Château-style New Potatoes (see page 139) and Hazelnut Galette with Peaches (see page 164)*

Goujons of Sole (see page 149); Sauce Rémoulade (see page 183) and Hungarian Nut Torte (see page 162)

NORMANDY-STYLE PHEASANT

This is an excellent way of cooking frozen pheasant. It can also be used very successfully with guinea fowl and chicken. The number of pheasants needed will depend on whether they will carve into 3 or 4 good portions each. If not roasters they will require longer cooking before the cream is added.

No. of servings	6	12	24	48
pheasant	2	3–4	6–8	12–16
flour, about	75 g/3 oz	150 g/5 oz	300 g/11 oz	600 g/1¼ lb
butter, unsalted	50 g/2 oz	100 g/4 oz	200 g/7 oz	400 g/14 oz
lard	50 g/2 oz	100 g/4 oz	200 g/7 oz	400 g/14 oz
onion, chopped	75 g/3 oz	150 g/5 oz	300 g/11 oz	600 g/1½ lb
celery, chopped	50 g/2 oz	100 g/4 oz	200 g/7 oz	400 g/14 oz
cooking apples, peeled and coarsely chopped	225 g/8 oz	450 g/1 lb	900 g/2 lb	1.8 kg/4 lb
dry cider	150 ml/¼ pint	300 ml/½ pint	600 ml/1 pint	1.2 litres/2 pints
double cream	60 ml/2½ fl oz	150 ml/¼ pint	300 ml/½ pint	600 ml/1 pint
salt and pepper	to taste	to taste	to taste	to taste

GARNISH *fried dessert apple rings and celery tufts*

Set the oven at moderate 180 c, 350 f, gas 4).

If the bird is large joint it into 4 portions, if small cook it whole. Clean the giblets and cover them with cold water and add seasoning, herbs and vegetables and make a stock (see page 32). Add the back of the carcass which has been jointed. Leave to simmer. Flour the joints or the whole bird and pat off the surplus. Melt the fat and fry the pheasant in the hot fat until golden. Remove and fry the onion and celery gently until softened. Add the apples and cook until well buttered. Draw the pan from the heat and stir in enough flour to absorb the fat. Gradually stir in the cider and the giblet stock. Bring to a simmer and add the pheasant and if necessary more stock to cover and season. Cover and simmer gently on the stove or place in the heated oven for about 1 hour or until tender.

When cooked, remove the pheasant and cook the sauce, uncovered, for 5 minutes or until slightly thickened. Mix a little of the sauce into the cream and stir the mixture into the pan. Adjust the seasoning.

Arrange the joints on a warmed deep serving dish and pour over the sauce. Garnish with unpeeled dessert apple rings fried golden in butter. Push little tufts of celery leaves through the centre of each ring.

Serve with Duchess or creamed potatoes and French beans or broccoli spears.

PARTRIDGE CASSEROLE WITH RED WINE AND CABBAGE

ILLUSTRATED ON PAGE 165

This traditional French dish from Normandy can be made with older partridge or grouse or with wood pigeon if partridge or grouse are out of season or too expensive.

No. of servings	6	12	24	48
partridge or grouse	3	6	12	24
or wood pigeon	6	12	24	48
streaky bacon	100 g/4 oz	200 g/7 oz	400 g/14 oz	800 g/1¾ lb
seasoned flour, for coating				
lard or bacon dripping	40 g/1½ oz	75 g/3 oz	150 g/5 oz	300 g/11 oz
onion, thinly sliced	150 g/5½ oz	300 g/11 oz	600 g/1½ lb	1.2 kg/3 lb
pickled pork belly, sliced	125 g/4½ oz	250 kg/9 oz	500 g/1 lb 2 oz	1 kg/2¼ lb
green cabbage, shredded	500 g/1 lb 2 oz	1 kg/2¼ lb	2 kg/4½ lb	4 kg/9 lb
salt and pepper	to taste	to taste	to taste	to taste
red wine	150 ml/¼ pint	300 ml/½ pint	600 ml/1 pint	1.2 litres/2 pints
game or white stock	150 ml/¼ pint	300 ml/½ pint	600 ml/1 pint	1.2 litres/2 pints
Frankfurter sausages	6	12	24	48

GARNISH *sprigs of watercress*

Set the oven at moderate (180 c, 350 f, gas 4).

Cover the breast of the birds with bacon, truss neatly and secure with string. Roll in seasoned flour and pat off the surplus. Heat the fat in a flameproof casserole or sauté pan and fry the onion and pickled pork, cut into neat pieces, until transparent. Add the birds and brown all over.

Remove the birds from the pan and put in a layer of cabbage. (If strong, the cabbage can be blanched first for 5 minutes in boiling salted water and drained.) Place the birds on top and cover with the remaining cabbage. Season to taste. Pour in the wine and stock, cover, bring to a simmer and place in the heated oven for 2 hours or until just tender. Check from time to time. If the liquid evaporates too much during cooking, add enough stock to cover the cabbage. Place Frankfurter sausages on top and cook for another 15–20 minutes. Adjust the seasoning, remembering that the pickled pork is salty.

When cooked, place the cabbage and birds on a warmed serving dish. Remove the string. Arrange the Frankfurters and pickled pork around the birds. If you are using pigeons, cut off the back to make stock and serve the breasts instead of the whole bird. Garnish with sprigs of watercress.

VEGETABLES AND SALADS

When selecting vegetables always be sure to choose only really fresh ones. Take care not to overcook them as this spoils their flavour and texture. Courgettes, marrow and cucumber casseroled with butter and fresh herbs are delicious and they are easy to cook in larger quantities. Potatoes cooked in a continental style add variety and interest to fish and meat dishes. Salads add colour and texture to cold meals and buffet menus and should, ideally, be made up from a variety of vegetables, fruits and nuts and should be attractively presented.

GLAZED CARROTS

ILLUSTRATED ON PAGE 48

This is the ideal accompaniment to veal or chicken blanquette. The carrots can be poached in the surplus veal or chicken stock.

No. of servings	6	12	24	48
carrots, preferably young	500 g/1 lb 1½ oz	1 kg/2¼ lb	2 kg/4½ lb	4 kg/9 lb
butter	25 g/1 oz	50 g/2 oz	100 g/4 oz	200 g/7 oz
sugar	15 g/½ oz	25 g/1 oz	50 g/2 oz	100 g/4 oz
good white stock, about	300 ml/½ pint	600 ml/1 pint	1 litre/1¾ pints	2 litres/3½ pints
salt and freshly ground black pepper	to taste	to taste	to taste	to taste

Peel and either slice the carrots or cut them, lengthwise, into small quarters. Put them into a wide saucepan with the butter and sugar and enough stock just to cover. Cover the pan and simmer for 20–25 minutes until just tender. Adjust the seasoning. Remove the lid and continue cooking until the liquid is reduced to a glaze. Take care at this stage that the carrots do not stick and burn. They should be bright and glistening when ready.

NOTE: *Do not cover the dish if you are keeping the carrots warm as the condensation will melt all the glaze away.*

Glazed Onions

Cook peeled button onions in the same way as the carrots, but simmer for 30 minutes before removing the lid.

CASSEROLED COURGETTES OR YOUNG MARROW

ILLUSTRATED ON PAGE 48

Courgettes should be used fresh as they become bitter if they are kept. The marrows should be young and tender and no longer than 30 cm/12 in. Butter and fresh herbs – mint, chives, chervil or parsley, summer savory or tarragon are essential for this delicious dish.

No. of servings	6	12	24	48
courgettes or	900 g/2 lb	1.8 kg/4 lb	3.5 kg/8 lb	7 kg/16 lb
young marrow	1.35 kg/2¾ lb	2.7 kg/6 lb	5.5 kg/12 lb	11.5 kg/24 lb
butter	75 g/3 oz	150 g/6 oz	300 g/12 oz	600 g/1¼ lb
salt and freshly ground black pepper	to taste	to taste	to taste	to taste
fresh mint, chives or parsley, summer savory, tarragon, mixed as available	25 g/1 oz	50 g/2 oz	100 g/4 oz	200/7 oz

Set the oven at cool (150c, 300f, gas 2) if casseroling the vegetables.

Top and tail the courgettes, but do not peel them. Cut them into thick slices. If you are using marrow, peel, deseed and cut it into 2.5-cm/1-in slices. (Discarding the seeds and pith.)

Generously butter a casserole, use a flameproof one if you are going to cook on a hob rather than in the oven. Put in the courgettes or marrow, season each layer, sprinkle with chopped herbs and dot with butter. Cover and cook gently over a low heat, stirring occasionally, or place in the heated oven and bake for 20–30 minutes until just tender.

ITALIAN-STYLE HARICOTS VERTS

ILLUSTRATED ON PAGES 126–7

The amount of garlic used in this recipe can be varied according to taste.

No. of servings	6	12	24	48
French beans	675 g/1½ lb	1.35 kg/3 lb	2.7 kg/6 lb	4.7 kg/12 lb
butter	50 g/2 oz	75 g/3 oz	150 g/5½ oz	300 g/11 oz
olive oil	2 tablespoons	3 tablespoons	6 tablespoons	180 ml/6 fl oz
garlic cloves, about	1–2	3–4	5–6	6–7
ground nutmeg	¼ teaspoon	½ teaspoon	1 teaspoon	1½ teaspoons
salt and freshly ground black pepper	to taste	to taste	to taste	to taste
Parmesan, grated	1 tablespoon	4 tablespoons	8 tablespoons	100 g/4 oz
fresh parsley, chopped	2 tablespoons	4 tablespoons	8 tablespoons	100 g/4 oz

Top and tail the beans and string if necessary. Simmer in boiling salted water until just tender. Drain and cover with a cloth to keep hot.

Heat the butter and oil in the pan. Chop the garlic and stir in with half the parsley and fry lightly. Add the beans, nutmeg and seasoning and mix over a moderate heat for about 5–10 minutes.

Mix in the grated Parmesan and serve at once sprinkled with the remaining parsley.

NOTE: *Runner beans may be cooked in the same way if they are prepared and then cut across into chunks.*

YOUNG BROAD BEANS WITH HERBS

It is essential to use young broad beans for this dish. The pods should be pale green and tender.

No. of servings	6	12	24	48
young broad beans	1.5 kg/3 lb	2.7 kg/6 lb	5.5 kg/12 lb	11 kg/24 lb
butter	75 g/3 oz	150 g/6 oz	250 g/10 oz	500 g/1¼ lb
fresh savory or mint, chopped, about	2 tablespoons	4 tablespoons	5 tablespoons	10 tablespoons

String any beans which need it. Chop across into 2-cm/1-in pieces and cook in boiling salted water for 12 minutes or until tender. Drain well. Melt the butter in the hot saucepan. Stir in the chopped fresh herbs, then mix in the beans and serve immediately.

BRUSSELS SPROUTS WITH CHESTNUTS

ILLUSTRATED ON PAGE 115

Choose tight sprouts for this dish. Fresh chestnuts are best, but canned whole chestnuts do save time. If you are using canned, drain them thoroughly before using.

No. of servings	6	12	24	48
chestnuts	450 g/1 lb	900 g/2 lb	1.8 kg/4 lb	3.5 kg/8 lb
stock, to cover				
Brussels sprouts	450 g/1 lb	900 g/2 lb	1.8 kg/4 lb	3.5 kg/8 lb
butter	75 g/3 oz	150 g/5½ oz	300 g/11 oz	600 g/1 lb 6 oz
salt and freshly ground black pepper	to taste	to taste	to taste	to taste

Slit one side of the chestnuts and roast them in a hot oven for 10 minutes until the skins split. Remove the peel and the inner skin. Heat the stock and simmer the chestnuts in it for 20 minutes or until tender. Drain.

Meanwhile, remove any discoloured leaves from the sprouts and trim the stalks. Wash, simmer in salted water for 10 minutes and drain thoroughly.

Melt the butter in a large thick pan and sauté the sprouts and chestnuts together until beginning to colour. Season to taste and serve as soon as possible.

CHESTNUT AND POTATO PURÉE

This is an excellent accompaniment to roast turkey, goose, duck and game. Canned chestnuts or puiée are a convenient alternative to fresh chestnuts, but they require more seasoning.

No. of servings	6	12	24	48
chestnuts, fresh	450 g/1 lb	900 g/2 lb	1.8 kg/4 lb	3.5 kg/8 lb
or canned chestnuts or unsweetened puiée	225 g/½ lb	450 g/1 lb	900 g/2 lb	1.8 kg/4 lb
stock	600 ml/1 pint	1 litre/1¾ pints	2 litres/3½ pints	4 litres/7 pints
potatoes	450 g/1 lb	900 g/2 lb	1.8 kg/4 lb	3.5 kg/8 lb
butter	25 g/1 oz	50 g/2 oz	100 g/4 oz	200 g/7 oz
single cream	75 ml/3 fl oz	150 ml/¼ pint	300 ml/½ pint	600 ml/1 pint
ground nutmeg	to taste	to taste	to taste	to taste
salt and finely ground black pepper	to taste	to taste	to taste	to taste
chopped celery heart	3 tablespoons	6 tablespoons	175 g/6 oz	350 g/12 oz

GARNISH *fried croûtons and celery leaves*

Set the oven at hot (220 c, 425 f, gas 7).

Slit the chestnut skins on one side and roast in the oven until they open. Peel off the outer and inner skins and boil the chestnuts in the stock for about 30 minutes until tender. Drain. If you are using canned chestnuts just drain off the liquid.

Peel the potatoes, put them in a pan of salted cold water and boil them until they are really soft. Drain them well and dry until floury.

Pass the chestnuts and potatoes through a mouli-légumes. Beat in the butter and cream and season well with nutmeg, black pepper and salt. Reheat over a moderate heat and just before serving mix in the crisp chopped, celery heart. Garnish with fried croûtons and fresh celery leaves.

Celeriac and Potato Purée

Make this as you would Chestnut and potato purée but using a celeriac root weighing about 450 g/1 lb for each 450 g/1 lb of chestnuts. Peel and cut up the celeriac put it into a pan of cold salted water and boil until tender. Drain. Purée with the boiled potatoes. Continue as in previous recipe.

Jerusalem Artichokes and Potato Purée

Substitute Jerusalem artichokes for the chestnuts. Put them into a pan of cold salted water, acidulated with a little lemon juice, boil and proceed as for Chestnut and potato purée. Mix in chopped fresh chervil or parsley instead of celery heart and garnish with fried croûtons.

*Rice and Cheese Croquettes (see page 24) and Devilled
Lamb Cutlets (see page 96)*

*Scallop and Artichoke Soup (see page 44) and Flemish
Carbonnade of Beef (see page 74)*

138

HASSELBACK POTATOES

ILLUSTRATED ON PAGE 116

This elegant version of roast potatoes is sometimes called fan potatoes. In the original recipe, Parmesan cheese is used but dry hard Cheddar can be substituted.

No. of servings	6	12	24	48
oval potatoes, medium sized	900 g/2 lb	2 kg/4 lb	3.5 kg/8 lb	7 kg/16 lb
butter or margarine	100 g/4 oz	200 g/7 oz	400 g/14 oz	800 g/1 lb 12 oz
salt	to taste	to taste	to taste	to taste
Parmesan cheese, grated	25 g/1 oz	50 g/2 oz	100 g/4 oz	200 g/7 oz
dried breadcrumbs	25 g/1 oz	50 g/2 oz	100 g/4 oz	200 g/7 oz

Set oven at moderately hot (200 c, 400 f, gas 6).

Peel potatoes. Cut them across into thin slices, but don't cut quite through so they still hold together, like the pages of a book. Place in a greased roasting tin. Sprinkle with salt and dot with knobs of butter. Bake for 30 minutes, basting occasionally. Meanwhile, mix together cheese and breadcrumbs. Remove the potatoes from the oven. Open the slices into a fan and sprinkle the cheese mixture liberally between the slices and over the top of the potatoes. Baste with butter and return to the oven for a further 20–30 minutes until golden and cooked through.

CHÂTEAU-STYLE NEW POTATOES

ILLUSTRATED ON PAGES 126–7

These are sometimes called Pommes rissolées. They are best made with new potatoes of uniform size, but you can also cut and shape maincrop potatoes.

No. of servings	6	12	24	48
new potatoes	900 g/2 lb	1.8 kg/4 lb	3.5 kg/8 lb	7 kg/15½ lb
butter	75 g/3 oz	125 g/5 oz	250 g/10 oz	1 kg/1¼ lb

GARNISH *chopped fresh mint or parsley*

Set oven at moderately hot (190 c, 375 f, gas 5).

Peel and blanche potatoes for 5 minutes in boiling salted water. Drain and dry. Heat butter in a large flameproof casserole, add potatoes and turn in the fat until coated. Cover and cook on top of the stove or in the oven for 20 minutes or until cooked and golden brown. Stir from time to time while cooking. Garnish.

POTATO GALETTE LYONNAISE

This savoury potato dish, flavoured with onion and cheese, is particularly suitable for preparing in advance. It also freezes very successfully.

No. of servings	6	12	24	48
potatoes	675 g/1½ lb	1.3 kg/3 lb	2.7 kg/6 lb	5.4 kg/12 lb
onions, sliced	350 g/12 oz	675 g/1½ lb	1.3 kg/3 lb	1.6 kg/6 lb
butter	100 g/4 oz	225 g/8 oz	450 g/1 lb	1 kg/2¼ lb
eggs, beaten	2	3	6	12
salt and freshly ground black pepper	to taste	to taste	to taste	to taste
ground nutmeg, optional	to taste	to taste	to taste	to taste
Cheddar cheese or Gruyère, grated	3 tablespoons	30 g/1½ oz	75 g/3 oz	175 g/6 oz

GARNISH *parsley sprigs*

Set oven at moderately hot (200 c, 400 f, gas 6).

Peel the potatoes. Put them in a pan of cold, salted water and boil them until they are cooked. Meanwhile, fry the onion in three-quarters of the butter until just beginning to colour.

Drain and dry the potatoes. Purée them. Mix in the fried onions with the butter. Add the beaten egg and season with salt, pepper and nutmeg if liked.

Turn into a shallow ovenproof dish, or dishes, smooth the top and cover with grated cheese and dot with the remaining butter.

The galette can be prepared ahead to this stage and then baked in the oven before it is served.

Place in the heated oven and bake for 20 minutes or until golden brown.

Garnish with parsley sprigs.

Freezing

Complete the cooking, cool and open freeze. Turn out onto freezer film, wrap closely and store in freezer. When required, remove freezer film, replace in ovenproof dish and defrost. Reheat in a moderately hot oven (200 c, 400 f, gas 6) for 30–45 minutes. If necessary protect the top with greaseproof paper to prevent over browning.

HOT POTATO SALAD

ILLUSTRATED ON PAGE 85

This salad can be made with new or small maincrop potatoes. It can be served for lunch with a mixed grill, chops or boiled ham.

No. of servings	6	12	24	48
potatoes	575 g/1¼ lb	1.1 kg/2¼ lb	2.3 kg/5½ lb	4.5 kg/11 lb
streaky bacon rashers	6	12	24	48
onion, chopped	2 tablespoons	4 tablespoons	8 tablespoons	400 g/14 oz
celery, chopped (optional)	50 g/2 oz	100 g/4 oz	200 g/7 oz	400 g/14 oz
gherkins, small, chopped	2	4	7	14
water	75 ml/3 fl oz	150 ml/6 fl oz	300 ml/½ pint	600 ml/1 pint
tarragon or wine vinegar	40 ml/1½ fl oz	75 ml/3 fl oz	150 ml/6 fl oz	300 ml/½ pint
sugar	1 teaspoon	2 teaspoons	1 tablespoon	2 tablespoons
salt	1 teaspoon	2 teaspoons	1 tablespoon	2 tablespoons
paprika	1 teaspoon	2 teaspoons	1 tablespoon	2 tablespoons

GARNISH *parsley or chervil*

Put the potatoes into well-salted cold water and boil them until tender. Skin and slice or cube them while still hot. Fry the chopped bacon slowly until crisp and the fat runs. Add the onion and celery and fry gently until coloured. Stir in the gherkin chopped into small pieces.

Mix together in a pan the water, vinegar, sugar and seasoning and bring them to the boil. Mix in the potatoes carefully and keep warm. Serve garnished with chopped parsley or chervil.

GREEK RICE SALAD

ILLUSTRATED ON PAGES 46–7

This salad looks particularly attractive when it is made in a ring mould. The centre of the ring can be filled with shellfish or cooked chicken in a Mousseline sauce.

No. of servings	6	12	24	48
rice, long grain	225 g/8 oz	450 g/1 lb	900 g/2 lb	1.8 kg/4 lb
Vinaigrette sauce approx. (page 182)	100 ml/4 fl oz	200 ml/7 fl oz	400 ml/14 fl oz	800 ml/1 pint 8 fl oz
chives or onions, finely chopped	2 tablespoons	4 tablespoons	50 g/2 oz	100 g/4 oz
dried basil or marjoram	½ teaspoon	1 teaspoon	2 teaspoons	4 teaspoons
parsley or fresh mint, chopped	2 tablespoons	4 tablespoons	50 g/2 oz	100 g/4 oz
green olives, chopped	1 tablespoon	2 tablespoons	4 tablespoons	100 g/4 oz
canned red pimentos	1	2	4	8
tomatoes	3	6	12	24
salt and black pepper	to taste	to taste	to taste	to taste
lemon juice	to taste	to taste	to taste	to taste

GARNISH *black and green olives, halved and stoned*

Cook the rice in plenty of boiling salted water until just cooked. Drain in a colander, cover with a dry cloth to absorb the steam and dry off.

Mix the Vinaigrette sauce using lemon juice or tarragon vinegar and add the chives, herbs and chopped olives. Mix into the rice while still warm. Cut 6 strips off the canned pimento, chop the remainder and mix into the rice.

Skin, seed and chop the tomatoes and add them to the rice. Season well with salt and black pepper and sharpen with lemon juice if required. Press the rice into a 20-cm/8-in ring mould with an 11-cm/4½-in cavity in the centre and leave to set.

Unmould by placing a serving dish on top of the rice ring and inverting it. A slight shake will loosen the rice. Garnish with black and green olives. (The mould does not need greasing because of the oil in the rice.)

WINTER SALAD

ILLUSTRATED ON PAGE 35

This salad can be prepared half a day in advance, covered with cling film and refrigerated until required.

No. of servings	6	12	24	48
SOURED CREAM DRESSING				
soured cream	200 ml/7 fl oz	400 ml/14 fl oz	800 ml/1 pint 8 fl oz	1.6 litres/2¾ pints
caster sugar, about	1½ teaspoons	1 tablespoon	2 tablespoons	4 tablespoons
mild French mustard	2 teaspoons	1 tablespoon	2 tablespoons	4 tablespoons
salt, about	½ teaspoon	1 teaspoon	2 teaspoons	4 teaspoons
lemon juice or tarragon vinegar	1 tablespoon	2 tablespoons	4 tablespoons	120 ml/4 fl oz
chicory heads	3	6	12	24
celery hearts	1–2	3–4	5–6	10
rosy dessert apples	3	6	12	24
lemon juice	as required	as required	as required	as required
cooked beetroot, small	1	2	4	8
GARNISH				
walnuts, shelled	50 g/2 oz	100 g/4 oz	225 g/7 oz	450 g/1 lb

First make the dressing so that the salad ingredients can be coated as soon as they are cut to prevent them from discolouring. Combine all the dressing ingredients in a mixing bowl and season to taste.

Discard any damaged chicory leaves and retain some good ones whole to line the serving bowl. Slice the heads, break them up and drop into the dressing.

Clean the celery hearts, chop and add them to the dressing. Wipe and core the apples. Cut some unpeeled slices to use for a garnish and brush them with lemon juice. Peel and chop the remainder and add to the dressing. Skin the beetroot, cut out balls with a French scoop and set aside. Chop the remainder and add to the dressing. Mix all the ingredients together.

Line a serving bowl with chicory leaves. Pile in the salad. Arrange the unpeeled apple slices in the centre as flower petals and garnish the salad with beetroot balls and walnuts. Cover closely and refrigerate.

COLESLAW

ILLUSTRATED ON PAGE 85

This popular white cabbage salad can be varied by the addition of a variety of ingredients such as pimento, apple, walnuts or peanuts. It can be dressed with either mayonnaise (see page 183) or soured cream dressing (see page 143).

No. of servings	6	12	24	48
white cabbage, medium	½	1	2	4
carrots, medium	1	2	4	8
onion, chopped finely	1½ tablespoons	3 tablespoons	6 tablespoons	175 g/6 oz
celery, chopped (optional)	2 tablespoons	4 tablespoons	5 tablespoons	150 g/5 oz
Mayonnaise or Soured cream dressing (pages 183 and 143), about	150 ml/¼ pint	300 ml/½ pint	600 ml/1 pint	1.2 litres/2 pints
paprika	½ teaspoon	1 teaspoon	2 teaspoons	4 teaspoons
salt and freshly ground black pepper	to taste	to taste	to taste	to taste
lemon juice	to taste	to taste	to taste	to taste

GARNISH *walnut halves; salted peanuts, chopped*

Clean the cabbage, discard any tough leaves and the stalk and shred finely. Peel and grate the carrot and add with the onion and celery to the cabbage. Mix thoroughly with the Mayonnaise or Soured cream dressing. Season with paprika, salt, pepper and lemon juice. Garnish with walnut halves or chopped salted peanuts. Chill before serving.

AVOCADO, CUCUMBER AND TOMATO SALAD

ILLUSTRATED ON PAGE 17

This makes a refreshing hors d'oeuvre, particularly in summer when fresh herbs are available. It is important to make a lemon-based French dressing (see page 182) and not a vinegar-based one, the basic vinaigrette.

No. of servings	6	12	24	48
sugar	2 teaspoons	1 tablespoon	2 tablespoons	4 tablespoons
Lemon French dressing (page 182)	150 ml/¼ pint	300 ml/½ pint	600 ml/1 pint	1.2 litres/2 pints
tomatoes, firm	450 g/1 lb	900 g/2 lb	1.8 kg/4 lb	3.5 kg/8 lb
cucumber	¾	1½	3	6
avocado, ripe	2	4	8	16
fresh parsley, chopped	1 tablespoon	2 tablespoons	4 tablespoons	50 g/2 oz
fresh mint, chopped	1 tablespoon	2 tablespoons	4 tablespoons	50 g/2 oz
fresh chives	1 tablespoon	2 tablespoons	4 tablespoons	50 g/2 oz

Add sugar to the French dressing and mix it well. Skin the tomatoes. Cut them into wedges, remove the seeds and core. Peel and cube the cucumber. Peel the avocados, remove the stone and slice them into a bowl. Pour the dressing over them immediately to prevent them from discolouring.

Add the tomatoes and cucumber pieces and mix carefully.

Spoon into individual coupes and sprinkle generously with fresh herbs. Chill well before serving.

Lentil or Haricot Bean Salad

This Middle Eastern recipe may be used as an hors d'oeuvre as well as a side salad.

No. of servings	6	12	24	48
olive oil	75 ml/3 fl oz	150 ml/¼ pint	350 ml/12 fl oz	700 ml/good pint
lemon juice	25 ml/1 fl oz	50 ml/2 fl oz	100 ml/4 fl oz	200 ml/8 fl oz
ripe tomatoes	2	4	450 g/1 lb	900 g/2 lb
black olives, stoned	4	8	150 g/5 oz	275 g/10 oz
spring onions	2	4	8	16
garlic, clove	2	4	8	16
brown lentils or haricot beans	225 g/8 oz	450 g/1 lb	900 g/2 lb	1.8 kg/4 lb
salt and pepper	to taste	to taste	to taste	to taste
cumin seed	2 teaspoons	4 teaspoons	8 teaspoons	5 tablespoons

GARNISH *stoned black olives; spring onion green; chopped fresh mint*

Mix the olive oil with the lemon juice. Skin, core and chop the tomatoes coarsely. Stone and chop the olives. Chop the white part of the spring onions, reserving the green leaves for garnish. Crush the garlic.

Soak the lentils or beans overnight and discard the water. Simmer in fresh water until tender adding salt after they have begun to soften. Drain and while still hot mix in all the prepared ingredients, including the cumin seeds. If you do this while hot the flavours will be absorbed better.

Mix well and adjust the seasoning with salt, freshly ground black pepper and lemon juice. Allow to marinate well before serving. Garnish with halved black olives, chopped green of spring onions and chopped fresh mint.

NOTE: *This can be served as an hors d'oeuvre. Top it with hard-boiled egg, arranging chopped white and sieved yolks attractively with anchovy fillets.*

DINNER AND COCKTAIL SAVOURIES

When served at the end of dinner, these are a peculiarly British contribution to the menu and popular on all-male occasions such as business lunches and stag dinners. They should be well-seasoned, very hot and served in small portions. They can also be served as finger-food at cocktail and wine parties. They are best presented freshly-made and quickly heated in batches rather than kept hot for any length of time.

CHICKEN LIVER CROSTINI

Crostini can either be fried or baked. They can be made from bread or from continental rusks (biscottes). If you can't buy fresh chicken livers then frozen are readily available. Sherry, vermouth, Marsala or a medium wine are all excellent in the sauce.

No. of servings	6	12	24	48
slices buttered bread or biscottes	6	12	24	48
chicken livers	225 g/8 oz	450 g/1 lb	900 g/2 lb	1.8 kg/4 lb
seasoned flour, about	3 tablespoons	6 tablespoons	180 g/6 oz	250 g/8 oz
bacon or ham, chopped	100 g/4 oz	200 g/7 oz	400 g/14 oz	800 g/1¾ lb
button mushrooms, sliced	50 g/2 oz	100 g/4 oz	200 g/7 oz	400 g/14 oz
sherry or vermouth	2 tablespoons	4 tablespoons	120 ml/4 fl oz	240 ml/8 fl oz
chicken stock or bouillon cube	4 tablespoons	120 ml/4 fl oz	240 ml/8 fl oz	480 ml/16 fl oz
single cream	4 tablespoons	120 ml/4 fl oz	240 ml/8 fl oz	480 ml/16 fl oz
salt and pepper	to taste	to taste	to taste	to taste
lemon juice	to taste	to taste	to taste	to taste

GARNISH *grated lemon rind; parsley, chopped; garlic, finely chopped*

Set the oven at hot (220 c, 425 f, gas 7).

To make the crostini, remove the crusts from the bread and place the slices in a hot oven until crisp, or warm the biscottes in a moderate oven (160 c, 325 f, gas 3). (If you prefer a richer dish, use unbuttered bread, cut the crust off and deep fry it. Drain on kitchen paper and keep warm.)

Clean the chicken livers, cut them into uniform-sized pieces and toss in seasoned flour. Heat the butter and fry the bacon quickly. Add the chicken livers and fry for about 3 minutes until stiffened.

Add the sliced mushrooms and fry for 2–3 minutes. Mix in the sherry or vermouth and stock and cook gently for 8–10 minutes. Add the cream to the chicken livers and heat through. Season with salt, pepper and lemon juice. Place the crostini on individual serving plates and pile on the chicken livers.

Garnish with grated lemon rind, chopped parsley and finely chopped garlic. Serve immediately.

GOUJONS OF SOLE OR PLAICE

ILLUSTRATED ON PAGE 128

These crispy little fingers of fish are served as an hors d'oeuvre, a light fish dish or a hot cocktail savory. Either Dover or lemon sole or large plaice can be used.

No. of servings	6	12	24	48
sole or plaice fillets, skinned	700 g/1½ lb	1.35 kg/3 lb	2.7 kg/6 lb	5.4 kg/12 lb
seasoned flour, for coating				
eggs, beaten, about	2	4	7	14
oil and water (half and half)	4 tablespoons	120 ml/4 fl oz	240 ml/8 fl oz	420 ml/16 fl oz
fresh breadcrumbs, about	100 g/4 oz	200 g/7 oz	350 g/12 oz	700 g/1½ lb
fat for deep frying				
salt	to taste	to taste	to taste	to taste
Sauce tartare or Rémoulade (page 183)	400 ml/14 fl oz	800 ml/1½ pints	1.6 litres/3 pints	3.2 litres/6 pints

GARNISH *lemon twists; parsley sprigs*

Wipe the fillets dry on kitchen paper. Cut diagonally into narrow strips about 8 cm/3 in long and 1.5 cm/½ in wide to make goujons. Pass through seasoned flour and shake off any surplus. Make an egg wash by thoroughly mixing together the beaten egg, oil and water. Dip in the goujons, drip off the surplus mixture, dip in the breadcrumbs and shake off any surplus crumbs. You can store any left over crumbs in an airtight jar labelled fishy crumbs for further use. They will keep for a few days.

Heat deep fat to 180 C (350 F), put the fish, a few at a time, into a frying basket and fry them in the fat until crisp and golden. Drain on kitchen paper, season lightly with salt and keep warm. Serve hot and garnish with lemon twists and parsley sprigs. Hand round Sauce tartare or Rémoulade sauce (see page 183) separately.

SAVOURY SAMOSAS

ILLUSTRATED ON PAGE 36

These crisp little fried puffs have a curry flavoured filling and are popular appetisers.
They can be cooked in advance and reheated in a hot oven. The filling can be varied
to include green peas, minced meat or fish.

No. of servings	6	12	24	48
plain flour	150 g/5 oz	300 g/11 oz	600 g/1¼ lb	1.2 kg/2½ lb
salt	to taste	to taste	to taste	to taste
clarified butter	1 tablespoon	1½ tablespoons	3 tablespoons	6 tablespoons
natural yogurt, about	120 ml/4 fl oz	240 ml/8 fl oz	480 ml/16 fl oz	900 ml/1½ pints
FILLING				
butter for frying				
onion, finely chopped	75 g/3 oz	150 g/5 oz	300 g/11 oz	600 g/1¼ lb
root ginger, fresh finely chopped	1½ teaspoons	1 tablespoon	2 tablespoons	3½ tablespoons
ground coriander	1 tablespoon	2 tablespoons	4 tablespoons	8 tablespoons
chilli powder (optional)	¼ teaspoon	½ teaspoon	1 teaspoon	1½ teaspoons
mashed potatoes	350 g/12 oz	700 g/1½ lb	1.4 kg/3 lb	2.8 kg/6 lb
garam masala or curry paste	2 teaspoons	1 tablespoon	2 tablespoons	3½ tablespoons
mango chutney	1½ tablespoons	3 tablespoons	90 ml/3 fl oz	180 ml/7 fl oz
salt	to taste	to taste	to taste	to taste

oil for frying
GARNISH *fresh fennel or fresh coriander; lemon twists*

Sieve the flour with the salt. Stir in the clarified butter and enough yoghurt to make a soft dough. Knead lightly on a floured board into a ball. Cover and leave to relax for at least 30 minutes.

Heat the butter and fry the onion in it until softened. Mix in the ginger, ground coriander and chilli powder if used, and fry lightly. Mix in the mashed potatoes and garam marsala. Finely chop up any lumps of mango in the chutney and add this. Cook gently until the liquid has evaporated and cool the mixture.

Roll out the dough as thinly as possible and cut it

into $6\frac{1}{2}$–7 cm/$2\frac{1}{2}$–$2\frac{3}{4}$ in squares. Put a spoonful of filling on one side of each square, dampen the edges, fold over into a triangle and press firmly.

Heat the oil to 180c, (350f) and fry a few samosas at a time, turning them as they plump and float to the surface. Fry them on both sides until they are crisp and golden in appearance.

Drain on kitchen paper and keep warm or set aside and reheat later in a hot oven (230c, 450f, gas 8). Garnish with fresh fennel leaves or fresh coriander and twists of lemon.

CROQUES-MONSIEUR

These crisp little fried sandwiches make a tasty savoury at the end of dinner and if you coat them with cheese sauce a satisfying supper dish.

No. of portions	6	12	24	48
bread slices (about 90 cm/3½ in square × 1 cm/½ in thick)	12	24	48	96
softened butter	75 g/3 oz	150 g/5 oz	300 g/11 oz	600 g/1¼ lb
slices of lean ham	4	8	16	32
Cheddar cheese or Gruyère, grated	100 g/4 oz	200 g/7 oz	400 g/14 oz	800 g/1¾ lb
oil for frying				

Remove the crusts from the bread and spread one side of each slice with butter and cover half the slices with a slice of ham and a layer of cheese. Top with the remaining slices of bread and press the sandwiches firmly together. Cut each one into three equal portions about the size of fingers.

Heat the oil and fry the fingers in it until golden brown, turning once. Drain on absorbent kitchen paper and serve hot, allowing 3 croques for each person.

SAVOURY EGG CROQUETTES

You can vary this recipe by adding chopped cooked chicken or flaked cooked smoked haddock. The croquettes can be prepared in advance and refrigerated or frozen either before or after frying. If they have been fried, they can be reheated in a hot oven (200 C, 400 F, gas 6) for 15–20 minutes.

No. of servings	6	12	24	48
PANADA				
butter	40 g/1½ oz	80 g/3 oz	160 g/5 oz	300 g/11 oz
onion, finely chopped	1 tablespoon	2 tablespoons	4 tablespoons	8 tablespoons
flour	40 g/1½ oz	80 g/3 oz	160 g/5 oz	300 g/11 oz
milk	150 ml/¼ pint	300 ml/½ pint	600 ml/1 pint	1.2 litres/2 pints
Cheddar cheese, grated	75 g/3 oz	150 g/5 oz	300 g/11 oz	600 g/1¼ lb
eggs, hard-boiled	6	12	24	48
cooked ham, chopped	100 g/4 oz	200 g/7 oz	400 g/14 oz	800 g/1¾ lb
parsley, chopped	2 tablespoons	4 tablespoons	8 tablespoons	16 tablespoons
lemon juice	to taste	to taste	to taste	to taste
salt and freshly ground black pepper	to taste	to taste	to taste	to taste
FOR COATING				
egg beaten	2	4	7	14
oil and water (half and half)	4 tablespoons	120 ml/4 fl oz	240 ml/8 fl oz	420 ml/14 fl oz
dried breadcrumbs	100 g/4 oz	200 g/7 oz	350 g/12 oz	700 g/1½ lb

fat for deep frying

GARNISH *parsley sprigs, deep fried or fresh*

Heat the butter and fry the onion gently in it until softened. Blend in the flour and then the milk. Simmer to form a thick sauce. Remove from the heat and stir in the cheese until melted. Shell and chop the eggs and add to the panada with the chopped ham and parsley. Season to taste with lemon juice, salt and freshly ground black pepper.

Spread the mixture out in a rectangular dish and leave to cool in the refrigerator. When cold and stiff divide into equal portions allowing two for each person. Roll into cork shapes on a lightly floured board. Coat twice with egg wash and crumbs. Leave the croquettes for a while until the coating is dry and set. Heat the oil. Arrange a few croquettes in the frying basket so they do not touch and fry in batches until golden and crisp. Drain on kitchen paper.

Serve garnished with deep-fried or fresh parsley sprigs. The croquettes can be cooked in advance and stored in the refrigerator or freezer. Reheat in a hot oven (200 c, 400 f, gas 6).

―――――――――VARIATIONS―――――――――

1 Replace ham with cooked finely flaked smoked haddock fillet or kipper fillets
2 Replace ham with very finely chopped cooked chicken or turkey
3 Replace ham with crisply fried chopped streaky bacon

STUFFED EGGS

ILLUSTRATED ON PAGE 36

This makes an attractive hors d'oeuvre or cocktail savoury. The filling can be varied in a number of different ways.

No. of servings	6	12	24	48
large eggs	6	12	24	48
red canned salmon, puréed	100 g/4 oz	225 g/8 oz	450 g/1 lb	900 g/2 lb
mayonnaise or double cream, about	3 tablespoons	6 tablespoons	150 ml/¼ pint	250 ml/½ pint
salt and freshly ground black pepper	to taste	to taste	to taste	to taste
anchovy essence	to taste	to taste	to taste	to taste
lemon juice	to taste	to taste	to taste	to taste

paprika

GARNISH *cress; radish roses*

Put the eggs into a frying basket in a large pan and cover them with cold water. Bring the water gently to the boil and simmer for 10 minutes. Crack the eggs and cool them under running cold water to prevent dark rings from forming round the yolks.

Shell the eggs, cut them in half horizontally and neatly remove the pointed end of each half egg to provide a flat base. Reserve this bit of egg white. Scoop out the egg yolks and sieve.

Mix the sieved egg yolk with the salmon purée and add enough mayonnaise or cream to bind to a stiff enough consistency so it can be piped. Season to taste with salt, freshly ground black pepper, anchovy essence and lemon juice.

Fill a forcing bag, fitted with a large nozzle, with the egg mixture and pipe it carefully into the egg white cups. Cap the filling with a small piece of egg white and sprinkle with paprika. (The cups can be lined with chopped cress before filling.) Arrange on a large plate or on individual small ones and garnish with cress and radish roses.

———————VARIATIONS———————

You can replace the salmon with an equal quantity of any of the following:
1 Sardine purée flavoured with cayenne pepper and lemon juice
2 Finely minced ham or cooked tongue seasoned with Worcestershire sauce or French mustard
3 Cream cheese flavoured with curry paste and lemon juice

*Mushrooms with Hazelnuts (see page 16) and Blanquette
of Veal (see page 92)*

*Cream of Vegetable Soup (see page 37) and Provençale-
style Red Mullet (see page 72)*

MUSHROOM PUFFS

ILLUSTRATED ON PAGE 36

These little Russian-style pastries can either be deep fried or glazed with beaten egg and baked for 15–20 minutes in a hot oven. They can be made in advance and refrigerated or frozen.

No. of servings	6	12	24	48
mushrooms	150 g/5 oz	300 g/11 oz	600 g/1¼ lb	1.2 kg/2½ lb
butter	25 g/1 oz	50 g/2 oz	100 g/4 oz	200 g/7 oz
onion, chopped	25 g/1 oz	50 g/2 oz	100 g/4 oz	200 g/7 oz
cream cheese	150 g/5 oz	300 g/11 oz	600 g/1¼ lb	1.2 kg/2½ lb
salt and freshly ground pepper	to taste	to taste	to taste	to taste
shortcrust pastry	250 g/8 oz	500 g/1 lb 2 oz	1 kg/2¼ lb	2 kg/4½ lb

oil for deep frying

GARNISH *dill wisps*

Rinse and dry the mushrooms. Chop the caps and stalks. Heat the butter and fry the onions and mushrooms lightly in it, mix in the cream cheese. Season well with salt and freshly ground black pepper. Allow to cool.

Roll the pastry out thinly and cut into 8–9 cm/3½–3¾ in squares. When making 24 or more portions, work up the trimmings and roll out to make more. Put a spoonful of filling on each square. Dampen the edges, fold over into triangles and press the edges neatly together using a crimper or a fork.

Heat the oil and deep fry the pastries until puffed and golden. Drain on kitchen paper.

Serve hot, garnished with sprigs of dill. Allow 2 for each person.

——————— VARIATIONS ———————

Instead of mushrooms you can use minced cooked haddock; canned salmon; tuna; crab or pilchards or chicken livers and bacon in the filling.

GÂTEAU ST HONORÉ

ILLUSTRATED ON PAGES 46-7

This party gâteau can also be served for tea or as a dessert at lunch or supper. The filling can either be whipped cream of Crème pâtissière (see page 189). If preferred, the base may be made with puff pastry instead of sweet shortcrust. Serve on the day it is made.

No. of servings	6	12	24	48
SWEET SHORTCRUST				
plain flour	100 g/4 oz	225 g/8 oz	450 g/1 lb	900 g/2 lb
butter	65 g/2½ oz	130 g/4½ oz	250 g/9 oz	500 g/1 lb 2 oz
caster sugar	2 teaspoons	4 teaspoons	2½ tablespoons	5 tablespoons
egg yolk	1	2	4	8
water, about	1 tablespoon	2 tablespoons	60 ml/2½ fl oz	120 ml/4 fl oz
CHOUX PASTRY				
butter	40 g/1½ oz	80 g/3 oz	160 g/5½ oz	320 g/11½ oz
water	150 ml/¼ pint	300 ml/½ pint	600 ml/1 pint	1.2 litres/2 pints
flour, sieved	75 g/3 oz	150 g/5½ oz	300 g/11 oz	600 g/1 lb 6 oz
eggs, beaten	2	4	8	16
FILLING				
cream, whipped	300 ml/½ pint	600 ml/1 pint	1.2 ml/2 pints	2.4 ml/4 pints
sherry or liqueur	to taste	to taste	to taste	to taste
CARAMEL TOPPING				
sugar	75 g/3 oz	150 g/5½ oz	350 g/12 oz	700 g/1½ lb
water	3 tablespoons	6 tablespoons	150 ml/¼ pint	300 ml/½ pints

DECORATION *crystallised rose and violet petals*

Sieve the flour and rub in the butter. Mix in the sugar. Beat the egg yolk with the water and stir it into the flour mixture. If the mixture seems too dry you may need to add a little more water. Work it into a soft not sticky dough and leave aside to relax.

To make the choux pastry: melt the butter in the water, bring it to the boil and add the flour. Beat until it is smooth over a low heat. Let the mixture cool slightly and very gradually beat in the eggs. This must be done carefully or the choux pastry will be too liquid. Prepare a forcing bag with a plain 1.5-cm/$\frac{3}{4}$-in nozzle and put the choux pastry into it.

Set the oven at hot (220c, 425f, gas 7).

Grease a baking sheet. Roll the shortcrust pastry out into a 20-cm/8-in circle. Place the pastry on the baking sheet and prick it all over.

Dampen the edge of the circle and pipe a ring of choux pastry onto the damp edge.

Prepare another baking sheet and pipe the remaining choux into small buns the same width as the ring onto it. Place the pastry base on the top shelf of the heated oven and the puffs below and bake for 15 minutes. Reduce the heat to moderately hot (190c, 375f, gas 5), reverse the baking trays and bake for a further 20 minutes or until cooked. Remove from the oven and cool on wire trays. Slit the choux ring and puffs on the side to allow the steam to escape.

Flavour the filling cream with sherry or liqueur.

Put this mixture into a forcing bag and pipe it into the choux ring and the puffs.

Melt the sugar for the caramel with a little water over a low heat. When completely dissolved boil briskly without stirring until a good caramel colour. Dip the base of the puffs into the caramel and fix on the ring. Pour the remaining caramel over the top of the puffs, one by one, and quickly sprinkle alternatively with rose and violet petals. Fill the centre of the ring with the remaining cream and decorate.

—————— VARIATION ——————

You can also fill the gâteau with a richer cream, a Crème St Honoré. First make a crème pâtissère (see page 189), flavour it with a liqueur and fold in egg whites whipped to soft peaks. Allow 2 egg whites for every 300 ml/$\frac{1}{2}$ pint of cream.

PROFITEROLES

These little choux puffs can be filled with whipped cream flavoured with liqueur or chocolate or coffee or crème pâtissière flavoured with rum.

No. of servings	6	12	24	48
choux pastry	as above	as above	as above	as above
crème pâtissière (page 189)	300 ml/$\frac{1}{2}$ pint	600 ml/1 pint	1.2 ml/2 pints	2.4 ml/4 pints
chocolate cream sauce	450 ml/$\frac{3}{4}$ pint	900 ml/1$\frac{1}{2}$ pints	1.8 ml/3 pints	3.6 ml/6 pints
egg wash				

Set the oven at hot (220c, 425f, gas 7).

Make the choux pastry as for the Gâteau St Honoré above using a forcing bag with a plain 1.5-cm/$\frac{1}{2}$-inch nozzle and pipe small buns on a floured baking tray leaving space for expansion. Remove and slit the side to allow the steam to escape and cool on a wire tray. Fill with whipped cream or Crème pâtissière (see page 189) using a forcing bag. Place in a pyramid in a large bowl or individual dishes allowing 5 profiteroles per portion. Pour over hot Chocolate cream sauce (see page 188) and serve immediately.

HUNGARIAN NUT TORTE

ILLUSTRATED ON PAGE 128

This continental torte is made with ground nuts instead of flour. Hazelnuts are best but walnuts or almonds can be used instead or a mixture. The crisp caramel topping should be put on the day the torte is served as it softens quickly. In summer it is particularly delicious filled with fresh raspberries, strawberries or peaches and cream. In winter you can use black cherry conserve and cream or butter cream.

No. of servings	6	12	24	48
number of tortes	1	2	4	8
eggs, separated	4	8	12	24
caster sugar	125 g/5 oz	250 g/8 oz	500 g/1 lb 2 oz	1 kg/2$\frac{1}{4}$ lb
nuts, shelled, ground	100 g/4 oz	250 g/8$\frac{3}{4}$ oz	450 g/1 lb	900 g/2 lb
FILLING				
cream, whipped	150 ml/$\frac{1}{4}$ pint	300 ml/$\frac{1}{2}$ pint	600 ml/1 pint	1.2 litres/2 pints
raspberries	225 g/8 oz	450 g/1 lb	900 g/2 lb	1.8 kg/4 lb
CARAMEL TOPPING (optional)				
sugar	75 g/3 oz	150 g/5$\frac{1}{2}$ oz	350 g/12 oz	700 g/1$\frac{1}{2}$ lb
water	3 tablespoons	6 tablespoons	150 ml/$\frac{1}{4}$ pint	250 ml/$\frac{1}{2}$ pint

DECORATION *whole raspberries or nuts and piped cream; or caramel topping and spun sugar (see below)*

Set the oven at moderate (180 c, 350 f, gas 4).

For each torte line the base and grease two 20-cm/8-in sandwich tins. Whisk together the egg yolks and the sugar until they turn a pale lemon colour. Fold in the nuts.

Whisk the egg whites until stiff but not brittle and fold them carefully into the mixture using a metal spoon. Spread evenly in the tins and place in the centre of the oven and bake for 30 minutes or until set and the top is springy. Remove from the oven and allow to shrink before turning out on a baking tray.

When the torte is cold, spread the bottom half with whipped cream, reserving a little for decoration, and cover it with raspberries. Place the other half of the torte on top. Decorate with piped cream and raspberries or caramel.

To make the caramel: put the sugar and water together in a pan and heat slowly to dissolve the sugar. Then boil briskly until it becomes caramel coloured. Using an oiled palette knife, spread the caramel evenly over the top of the torte and decorate at once. Before the topping hardens mark the torte with the back edge of the oiled palette knife into 6 equal portions so as to make serving easier. Cook the caramel remaining in the pan a bit more and trickle it over the decoration or use the palette knife to pull it into spun sugar and spin it over the torte.

PINEAPPLE AND CHERRY FLAN

ILLUSTRATED ON PAGES 86–7

This continental pâtisserie can be filled with any combination of canned or fresh fruit.
Two contrasting colours arranged in circles or wedges produce the best effect. The
pastry case and the crème pâtissier can be made in advance, but the flan should not
be filled until the day on which it is to be eaten.

No. of servings	6	12	24	48
SWEET SHORTCRUST				
butter or shortening	75 g/3 oz	150 g/5½ oz	300 g/11 oz	600 g/1¼ lb
plain flour	175 g/6 oz	350 g/12 oz	700 g/1½ lb	1.4 kg/3¼ lb
caster sugar	2 teaspoons	4 teaspoons	60 g/2 oz	120 g/4½ oz
egg yolks	1	2	4	8
water, to mix				
Crème pâtissière (page 189)	300 ml/½ pint	600 ml/1 pint	1.2 litres/2 pints	2.4 litres/4 pints
lemon juice or vanilla	to taste	to taste	to taste	to taste
cherries, stoned	225 g/8 oz	450 g/1 lb	900 g/2 lb	1.8 kg/4 lb
pineapple slices, small, about	8	16	32	64
GLAZE				
apricot jam	100 g/4 oz	200 g/7 oz	400 g/14 oz	800 g/1¾ lb
water	1 tablespoon	2 tablespoons	4 tablespoons	120 ml/4 fl oz
lemon juice	1 tablespoon	2 tablespoons	4 tablespoons	120 ml/4 fl oz

Set the oven at moderately hot (190 c, 375 f, gas 5).

Rub the fat into the flour and mix in the sugar. Beat the egg yolk with a little water and stir it into the mixture. Work the ingredients into a soft but not sticky dough, adding a little extra water if required. Leave to relax in a cool place for at least 30 minutes.

Roll the pastry out thinly and use to line a 20-cm/8-in flan ring. Bake blind and cool.

Flavour the cold crème pâtissier with lemon juice or vanilla and spread evenly in the flan case. Arrange the pineapple slices and the cherries in an attractive pattern on top of it.

To make the glaze: dissolve the jam with the water and sieve it. Add the lemon juice, bring the mixture to the boil and spoon it carefully over the fruit until evenly coated. Brush the edge of the flan with the remaining glaze.

HAZELNUT GALETTE WITH PEACHES

ILLUSTRATED ON PAGES 126–7

This continental-style galette should be served very crisp. The hazelnut crust can be made in advance but the caramel topping and fruit and cream filling should be left until shortly before the galette is to be eaten. Fresh apricots, raspberries or strawberries can be used instead of peaches.

No. of servings	6	12	24	48
number of galettes	1	2	4	8
hazelnuts	175 g/6 oz	350 g/12 oz	700 g/1½ lb	1.4 kg/3 lb
plain flour, sieved	200 g/7 oz	400 g/14 oz	800 g/1¾ lb	1.6 kg/3½ lb
caster sugar	75 g/3 oz	150 g/5½ oz	300 g/11 oz	600 g/1¼ lb
butter	115 g/4 oz	230 g/8 oz	460 g/1 lb	920 g/2 lb
FILLING				
fresh peaches, about	6	12	24	48
whipping cream	350 ml/12 fl oz	700 ml/1¼ pints	1.4 litres/2½ pints	2.8 litres/4¾ pints
caster sugar	to taste	to taste	to taste	to taste
CARAMEL TOPPING				
sugar	100 g/4 oz	200 g/7 oz	400 g/14 oz	800 g/1¾ lb

Set the oven at moderate (180 C, 350 F, gas 4).

For each galette spread the hazelnuts in a baking tin and roast them under a grill or in a hot oven. Rub off the skins. Roughly chop 25 g/1 oz, for each galette and grind the remainder.

Mix the flour with the ground nuts and sugar. Rub in the butter as you would for a shortcrust pastry. Knead into a smooth dough and chill for 30 minutes or until firm. Shape into a thick cylindrical shape and divide equally into 4. Roll out each piece into a circle. Grease a baking sheet and using a fish slice lift the circles onto it. Prick them to prevent them from blistering. Place in the heated oven and bake for 15–20 minutes until coloured and set. Remove from the oven and cool.

Scald the peaches and peel them. Halve them, remove their stones and slice them evenly. Whip the cream until firm peaks form and sweeten.

To make the caramel: dissolve the sugar thoroughly with a little water over a low heat and then boil it briskly, without stirring, until it becomes a rich caramel colour.

Pour the caramel over one of the biscuit circles and spread it evenly with an oiled palette knife. Before the caramel sets arrange a flower pattern with 6–8 peach slices in the centre and sprinkle on the chopped nuts, trickle caramel over the fruit.

Spread the remaining biscuits with whipped cream and cover with sliced peaches. Pile them on top of each other and place the decorated biscuit on the top.

ABOVE: *Partridge Casserole with Red Wine and Cabbage (see page 130) and Orange Cup Puddings (see page 177)*
OVERLEAF: *Cucumber and Green Pea Soup (see page 50); Coq au Vin (see page 108) and Old-Fashioned English Trifle (see page 172)*

Dressed Crab (see page 56); Pork and Apple Guizot (see page 81) and Leek and Cream Tarts (see page 22)

APRICOT CHARLOTTE RUSSE

ILLUSTRATED ON PAGE 48

This is a pretty, decorative sweet for the buffet table and in this luxury version liqueur-flavoured whipped cream and fruit replace the usual filling of Bavarian custard cream. In summer, fresh strawberries and raspberries are particularly delicious, and in winter canned apricots, peaches and mandarines are preferable to canned or frozen berries which are too soft and wet. If you do not have angelica, use halved green glacé cherries or grapes instead for decorating. It is best to make this the day before it is to be eaten so that it can be refrigerated overnight.

No. of servings	6	12	24	48
canned sliced apricots in syrup	400 g/14 oz	800 g/1¼ lb	1.6 kg/3½ lb	3.2 kg/7 lb
packet lemon jelly (about 135 g/4½ oz each	1	2	4	8
angelica	20 g/¾ oz	30 g/1½ oz	50 g/2 oz	100 g/4 oz
whipping cream	300 ml/½ pint	600 ml/1 pint	1.2 litres/2 pints	2.4 litres/4 pints
apricot brandy (or other liqueur), about	3 tablespoons	6 tablespoons	180 ml/6 fl oz	350 ml/12 fl oz
Boudoir biscuits	18 75 g/3 oz	36 150 g/5½ oz	72 300 g/11 oz	144 600 g/1¼ lb

For each charlotte you will need a 1-litre/1¾-pint mould, which will serve 6.

Drain the fruit and measure the syrup. Dissolve the jelly in half the normal quantity of boiling water, add the fruit syrup and make up to the full quantity with cold water. (If you are using fresh fruit, replace the syrup with cold water.) Rinse the mould out with cold water, pour in a thin layer of liquid jelly and put into the refrigerator until set.

Arrange apricot slices and angelica diamonds in an attractive pattern on the set jelly base, dipping each piece of fruit in liquid jelly. Refrigerate and when the pattern is firmly fixed, cover with a layer of jelly and return to the refrigerator.

Whip the cream and flavour it with the liqueur. Trim off the round edges of the Boudoir biscuits.

Dip them one at a time into liquid jelly and stand them closely together round the inside edge of the mould, sugared side outwards. Fill the centre with layers of whipped cream and sliced fruit, beginning and ending with cream.

Pour some of the remaining jelly gradually down the sides of the mould between the biscuits until they have absorbed it and the liquid jelly shows at the top rim of the mould. Chill the charlotte in the refrigerator until required. Trim any biscuits which are higher than the rim of the mould with scissors. Any remaining jelly can be poured into a shallow dish and left to set.

Unmould carefully onto a serving plate. Decorate with the remaining whipped cream, chopped jelly and extra fruit as desired.

SAVARIN AU RHUM

ILLUSTRATED ON PAGES 18

This is a popular dessert which looks very attractive on the buffet table. In summer it can be decorated with fresh strawberries and sliced berries folded into a Crème Chantilly filling.

No. of servings	6	12	24	48
plain strong flour	125 g/4½ oz	250 g/9 oz	450 g/1 lb	900 g/2 lb
salt	¼ teaspoon	½ teaspoon	¾ teaspoon	1½ teaspoons
fresh yeast or	10 g/¼ oz	15 g/½ oz	25 g/1 oz	50 g/2 oz
dried yeast	1½ teaspoons	3 teaspoons	2 tablespoons	4 tablespoons
caster sugar	25 g/1 oz	50 g/2 oz	100 g/4 oz	200 g/7 oz
warm water	50 ml/2 fl oz	100 ml/4 fl oz	200 ml/7 fl oz	400 ml/14 fl oz
eggs, beaten	2	4	8	16
butter, creamed	65 g/2½ oz	125 g/4½ oz	250 g/9 oz	500 g/1 lb 2 oz
RUM SYRUP				
sugar	150 g/5½ oz	300 g/11 oz	450 g/1 lb	900 g/2 lb
water	250 ml/8 fl oz	500 ml/17 fl oz	1 litre/1¾ pint	2 litres/3½ pints
rum or kirsch	4 tablespoons	120 ml/4 fl oz	240 ml/8½ fl oz	500 ml/17 fl oz
APRICOT GLAZE				
apricot jam	200 g/7 oz	400 g/14 oz	800 g/1¾ lb	1.6 kg/3½ lb
lemon juice	1 tablespoon	2 tablespoons	60 ml/2 fl oz	120 ml/4 fl oz
water	1 tablespoon	2 tablespoons	60 ml/2 fl oz	120 ml/4 fl oz

DECORATION *glace cherries; angelica diamonds or fresh fruit and cream*

Grease savarin ring moulds. Use 17-cm/7-in moulds for 6 portions, or 23-cm/9-in ones for 12 portions.

Sieve the flour and salt into a bowl and put to warm. Blend the fresh yeast with the sugar and warm water, add beaten eggs, (if using dried yeast, dissolve it with the sugar in the warm water and leave it to froth about 20 minutes, before adding the eggs).

Make a well in the flour, gradually stir in the yeast liquid and beat it into a smooth batter. Cover and leave to prove in a warm place for 45 minutes or until the dough has doubled in bulk. Gradually beat in the creamed butter. Half fill the savarin moulds and leave in a warm place until the dough rises to the rim.

Set the oven at moderately hot (200 C, 400 F, gas 6).

Place the moulds in the heated oven and bake for 10 minutes. Reduce the heat to moderate (180 c, 350 f, gas 4) and continue cooking for 30 minutes or until a skewer inserted into the savarins comes out clean. Remove from the oven and allow to cool for 5 minutes. Loosen the edges with a knife and unmould upside down. Leave to cool.

To make the syrup: dissolve the sugar in the water and boil it for 2 minutes. Remove from the heat and add rum or kirsch. When the savarin is cold, prick it and spoon over the syrup. Baste with any syrup which overflows until all of it is absorbed.

Decorate with glacé cherries and angelica leaves cut into diamond shapes.

Make the apricot glaze: dissolve the jam with the lemon juice and water, over gentle heat. Sieve, boil up and pour over the savarin. Fill with fresh or candied fruits and decorate, with piped whipped cream.

RICH CHOCOLATE PUDDING

This delicious rich chocolate pudding has a remarkably light texture. It can be served either hot or cold.

No. of servings	6	12	24	48
plain chocolate	100 g/4 oz	200 g/7 oz	400 g/14 oz	800 g/1¾ lb
butter or margarine	75 g/3 oz	150 g/5½ oz	300 g/11 oz	600 g/1¼ lb
milk	450 ml/¾ pint	900 ml/1½ pints	1.8 litres/3 pints	3.6 litres/6 pints
caster sugar	100 g/4 oz	200 g/7 oz	400 g/14 oz	800 g/1¾ lb
vanilla essence	¼ teaspoon	½ teaspoon	1 teaspoon	1½ teaspoons
eggs, separated	3	6	12	24
fresh white breadcrumbs	200 g/7 oz	400 g/14 oz	800 g/1¾ lb	1.6 kg/3½ lb

Melt the chocolate with the butter in a bowl over hot water. Remove from the heat and stir until smooth. Heat the milk with the sugar and stir it into the chocolate. Add the vanilla to the beaten egg yolks and blend into the chocolate mixture. Add the breadcrumbs. Whisk the egg whites until stiff but not brittle and fold into the mixture.

For 6 servings, grease a 1.25-litre/2-pint pudding basin or mould. Use a larger one for a larger pudding, allowing room for the pudding to rise. Pour in the chocolate mixture. Cover with a plastic lid or greased foil, and secure firmly. Put into a saucepan containing enough simmering water to come half way up the bowl. Put the lid on the pan and cook over a gentle heat for about 2 hours, topping up with boiling water if necessary, until the pudding is well risen and spongy to the touch. Allow the pudding to shrink slightly before unmoulding it into a warm serving plate.

Serve hot with hot Chocolate cream sauce (see page 188) or cold with Crème Chantilly (see page 188).

OLD-FASHIONED ENGLISH TRIFLE

ILLUSTRATED ON PAGES 166–7

This is an excellent traditional English party sweet. Instead of being topped with cream, as is more common nowadays, it is covered in syllabub.

No. of servings	6	12	24	48
trifle sponges	4	8	16	32
macaroons or ratafia biscuits	25 g/1 oz	50 g/2 oz	100 g/4 oz	200 g/7 oz
Madeira or sweet sherry	75 ml/3 fl oz	150 ml/¼ pint	300 ml/½ pint	600 ml/1 pint
brandy (optional)	2 tablespoons	4 tablespoons	120 ml/4 fl oz	240 ml/8 fl oz
apricot conserve	100 g/4 oz	200 g/7 oz	400 g/14 oz	800 g/1¾ lb
CUSTARD				
egg yolks	2	4	8	16
cornflour	1 tablespoon	2 tablespoons	4 tablespoons	8 tablespoons
milk and single cream (half and half)	300 ml/½ pint	600 ml/1 pint	1.2 litres/2 pints	2.4 litres/4 pints
caster sugar, about	40 g/1½ oz	80 g/3 oz	160 g/5½ oz	320 g/11½ oz
vanilla essence	to taste	to taste	to taste	to taste
SYLLABUB				
lemon	1	2	4	8
Madeira or sweet white wine	100 ml/3½ fl oz	200 ml/7 fl oz	400 ml/14 fl oz	800 ml/1¼ pints
caster sugar, about	50 g/2 oz	100 g/4 oz	200 g/7 oz	400 g/14 oz
double cream	300 ml/½ pint	600 ml/1 pint	1.2 litres/2 pints	2.4 litres/4 pints

DECORATION *ratafia biscuits and angelica diamonds*

Split the trifle sponges and place a layer over the base of a glass bowl, interspersed with macaroons or ratafia biscuits. Mix together the Madeira and brandy and use half to soak the sponges and the macaroons. Spread with apricot conserve and cover with the remaining sponges. Soak with the rest of the wine mixture.

Make the custard by whisking up the egg yolks together with the cornflour. Mix the milk and cream, heat to boiling point and whisk into the eggs. Return to the pan and heat, stirring, until thickened, taking care not to boil or the mixture will curdle. Add a few drops of vanilla essence. Pour over the sponges and chill until set.

To make the syllabub: grate the zest off the lemon very finely, squeeze the juice from the lemon. Mix the wine with the lemon juice, the caster sugar, the lemon rind and leave to infuse. Strain out the zest. Gradually add the cream, whisking steadily until it peaks. Taste and adjust the sweetness if necessary. Cover the top of the trifle with the syllabub. Decorate with ratafia biscuits and angelica diamonds.

NOTE: *Syllabub is a pudding in its own right. It is generally served in individual goblets as a wine whip. It can be decorated with crushed praline or chopped pistachio nuts.*

LEMON FLUMMERY

ILLUSTRATED ON PAGE 58

This simple traditional old recipe makes a very pleasant change from custard to serve with baked pears and apples or stewed fruit.

No. of servings	6	12	24	48
water	300 ml/½ pint	600 ml/1 pint	1.2 litres/2 pints	2.4 litres/4 pints
butter	25 g/1 oz	50 g/2 oz	100 g/4 oz	225 g/8 oz
finely grated rind and lemon juice	1	2	4	8
plain flour	25 g/1 oz	50 g/2 oz	100 g/4 oz	225 g/8 oz
caster sugar	100 g/4 oz	225 g/8 oz	450 g/1 lb	900 g/2 lb
eggs, separated	1	2	4	8

Heat the water with the butter and grated lemon rind. Mix the flour and sugar in a bowl, gradually stir in the hot liquid and beat until smooth. Beat the egg yolks and blend some of the cooked mixture with the beaten egg yolk and stir it back into the rest of the warm mixture. Pour it all into a saucepan, add the lemon juice and simmer gently for 5 minutes, stirring steadily. Pour into a cold bowl and cool. Whisk the egg white until stiff but not brittle and fold it into the cooled mixture.

Serve warm or cold as required.

SWEET ALMOND SAMOSAS

These little pastries have an almond paste filling. They are deep fried and then dipped into syrup prepared with orange-flavoured water.

No. of servings	6	12	24	48
PSTRY				
plain flour	175 g/6 oz	350 g/12 oz	700 g/1½ lb	1.4 kg/3 lb
butter	25 g/1 oz	50 g/2 oz	100 g/4 oz	200 g/7 oz
natural yoghurt, about	25 ml/1 fl oz	50 ml/2 fl oz	100 ml/4 fl oz	200 ml/7 fl oz
warm water, to mix				
FILLING				
caster sugar	20 g/¾ oz	40 g/1½ oz	80 g/3 oz	160 g/5½ oz
ground cinnamon	pinch	¼ teaspoon	½ teaspoon	1 teaspoon
ground almonds	40 g/1½ oz	80 g/3 oz	160 g/5½ oz	320 g/11 oz
lemon juice	1 teaspoon	2 teaspoons	4 teaspoons	2 tablespoons
SYRUP				
sugar	225 g/8 oz	225 g/8 oz	450 g/1 lb	900 g/2 lb
water	300 ml/½ pint	450 ml/¾ pint	600 ml/1 pint	1.2 litres/2 pints
orange-flower water, a few drops				

Sift the flour and rub in the butter to the stage where fine breadcrumbs are formed. Mix in the yoghurt and enough warm water to make a soft, but not sticky dough. Knead gently, cover and leave to rest for 30 minutes.

Mix caster sugar, cinnamon and ground almonds together. Add lemon juice and knead mixture into a ball.

Roll dough out as thinly as possible and cut it into 5.5 cm/2¼ in squares. Break off small pieces of almond paste and place on one side of each square. Brush edges with water, fold over into triangles and press edges firmly together using fingertips.

To make the syrup: dissolve the sugar in the water and boil steadily until thickened and syrupy. Mix in a few drops of orange-flower water. Keep warm while frying the samosas.

Heat the oil to moderate (185 C, 365 F), and fry the samosas a few at a time until golden brown. Drain them on kitchen paper and plunge them into the syrup. Remove them quickly and serve hot and crisp. Alternatively, they can be soaked in the syrup for 5 minutes and served cold. They will be sweeter and softer.

PEARS BAKED IN CIDER

ILLUSTRATED ON PAGE 58

Comice pears are the ones with the best shape, but the taller thinner conference pears can also be used. They should be slightly under-ripe so that they retain their shape during baking.

No. of servings	6	12	24	48
cider	300 ml/½ pint	600 ml/1 pint	1.2 litres/2 pints	2.4 litres/4 pints
sugar	125 g/4 oz	225 g/8 oz	450 g/1 lb	900 g/2 lb
cinnamon sticks, (5-cm/2-in piece)	1	1	2	4
piece of lemon zest	1	2	4	8
firm dessert pears, medium sized	6	12	24	48

Set the oven at moderate (180 c, 350 f, gas 4).

Put the cider, sugar, cinnamon and lemon zest in a flameproof casserole and heat until the sugar has dissolved.

Cut a thin slice off the base of the pears so that they will stand upright. Peel the pears, leaving the stalks intact. Arrange them in the casserole which should be just large enough to take them. Place in the heated oven, cover and bake for 45–60 minutes until just tender when tested with a skewer. Place the pears upright in a deep serving dish using a slotted spoon. Boil up the cider syrup until reduced by half and strain it over the pears.

Serve hot or cold with Lemon flummery (see page 173) or clotted cream.

JALEBIS

ILLUSTRATED ON PAGE 75

These crisp fritter rings are sweetened with a syrup flavoured with orange-flower water.
To allow the flour to expand and lighten the batter, the mixture should stand
overnight before frying. Indian cooks use curds instead of yoghurt. They leave them
to ferment overnight and then do not need to use baking powder.

No. of servings	6	12	24	48
BATTER				
plain flour	75 g/3 oz	150 g/5½ oz	350 g/12 oz	700 g/1½ lb
baking powder	½ teaspoon	1 teaspoon	2 teaspoons	4 teaspoons
natural yoghurt	1½ tablespoons	3 tablespoons	6 tablespoons	180 ml/6 fl oz
water, about	75 ml/3 fl oz	150 ml/¼ pint	300 ml/½ pint	600 ml/1 pint
oil for frying				
SYRUP				
sugar	225 g/8 oz	350 g/12 oz	450 g/1 lb	575 g/1¼ lb
water	350 ml/½ pint	600 ml/1 pint	1 litre/1¾ pints	1.5 litres/2¾ pints
orange-flower water, a few drops				
Jalebis powder *or saffron*	to taste	to taste	to taste	to taste

DECORATION *toasted sesame seeds or desiccated coconut or chopped pistachio nuts*

Sift the flour and baking powder into a bowl. Mix in the yoghurt and enough water to make a batter the consistency of thick pouring cream. Beat until smooth and leave overnight in a warm place.

Dissolve the sugar in the water and boil steadily until thick and syrupy. Flavour with orange-flower water and jalebi powder or saffron. Keep warm.

Heat 3 cm/1¼ in of oil in a large frying pan to moderately hot (190 c, 375 f). Warm the batter slightly, stirring steadily. If it is too thin, mix a spoonful of flour with a little cold water and stir it into the batter.

Fill a small thin funnel with a little batter, holding the tip of the forefinger over the opening. Remove the finger long enough to pipe a circle or snail of batter into the oil. Close the funnel quickly by replacing the finger. Fry a few jalebis at a time for a few minutes, turning them once. Fry until crisp and golden on both sides. Remove with a perforated spoon and drop into the syrup for 4–5 minutes. Spread on a tray or plate and sprinkle with toasted sesame seeds or desiccated coconut or chopped pistachio nuts. If you like them crisp, then serve them hot, otherwise serve them cold with cream.

ORANGE CUP PUDDINGS

ILLUSTRATED ON PAGE 165

Cup puddings have been an English favourite since Mrs Beeton's day. They are very useful when catering for large numbers as they are cooked in invidual moulds and can either be baked or steamed in the oven.

No. of servings	6	12	24	48
oranges, medium	1–2	3	5	10
golden syrup	3 tablespoons	6 tablespoons	12 tablespoons	24 tablespoons
butter or margarine	150 g/5½ oz	350 g/12 oz	700 g/1½ lb	1.4 kg/3 lb
caster sugar	150 g/5½ oz	350 g/12 oz	700 g/1½ lb	1.4 kg/3 lb
eggs, beaten	3	6	12	24
plain flour	150 g/5½ oz	350 g/12 oz	700 g/1½ lb	1.4 kg/3 lb
baking powder	2 teaspoons	4 teaspoons	2 tablespoons	4 tablespoons
warm water, about	2 tablespoons	4 tablespoons	120 ml/4 fl oz	240 ml/8 fl oz

Set the oven at moderate (180 c, 350 F, gas 4).

Grease 6 100-ml/4-oz dariole moulds. Grate the orange rind finely and keep. Peel the orange, remove the pith and divide it into segments. Warm the golden syrup and spread 1 teaspoonful in the base of each dariole mould and arrange 2 orange segments on top.

Cream the butter and sugar with the grated orange rind until light and fluffy. Gradually beat in the eggs, folding in a little flour. Sieve the baking powder into the rest of the flour and add it to the mixture. This will prevent the mixture curdling. Add enough warm water to produce a soft dropping consistency.

Fill the dariole moulds two-thirds full, allowing room for the puddings to rise. Put them on a baking sheet and place them in the heated oven to bake for 25 minutes or until well risen and golden. Test with a skewer and remove from the oven. If necessary, trim the tops level, allow the puddings to shrink slightly and invert onto a warm serving plate. Serve with Orange foam sauce (see page 188).

Steamed Cup Puddings

Set the oven at moderately hot (190 c, 375 F, gas 5).

Make the puddings as you would baked ones but place them in a roasting tin with enough water to come half way up the moulds. This serves as a bain-marie. Cover the tin with a sheet of buttered greaseproof paper. Place in the heated oven and bake for about 50 minutes until set and golden. Test if the pudding is cooked by inserting a skewer. When it comes out clean the pudding is cooked. Serve hot with Orange foam sauce (see page 188).

COLD FRUIT SOUFFLÉ

*This light refreshing dessert can either be made with fruit juice, such as orange,
lemon or grapefruit, or with a purée of fresh or canned fruit – raspberries,
loganberries or apricots are the most successful.
For special occasions it can be flavoured with the appropriate liqueur– orange
Curacao, Cointreau or Grand Marnier for the citrus fruits, Kirsch for the berries and
Apricot Brandy for the apricots.*

No. of servings	6	12	24	48
eggs, separated	4	8	16	32
caster sugar	275 g/10 oz	550 g/1 lb 3 oz	1 kg/2¼ lb	2 kg/5 lb
orange juice	150 ml/¼ pint	300 ml/½ pint	600 ml/1 pint	1.2 litres/2 pints
lemon juice	75 ml/3 fl oz	150 ml/¼ pint	300 ml/½ pint	600 ml/1 pint
powdered gelatine	15 g/½ oz	30 g/1 oz	60 g/2 oz	120 g/4 oz
whipping cream	450 ml/¾ pint	900 ml/1½ pints	1.8 litres/3 pints	3.6 litres/6 pints
Cointreau (optional)	3 tablespoons	6 tablespoons	180 ml/6 fl oz	360 ml/12 fl oz

DECORATION *whipped cream; crystallised orange and lemon slices; pistachio nuts*

Choose the right sized soufflé dish so that the soufflé will stand 3–4 cm/1¼–1½ in above the dish. For a 4 egg soufflé (6 portions) use a 900-ml/1½-pint soufflé dish and for an 8 egg soufflé, a 1.75-litre/3-pint dish. It is not practical to serve the soufflés in larger containers.

Tie a band of double greaseproof paper around the outside of the soufflé dish. It should overlap by 5 cm/2 in and stand 3 cm/1¼ in above the dish.

Whisk the egg yolks, sugar and fruit juice together in a large bowl over a saucepan of simmering water until the mixture is thick enough to fall in ribbons from the whisk. Remove from the heat.

Thoroughly dissolve the gelatine in a few spoonfuls of boiling water and whisk into the mixture. Set aside to cool. Whisk the egg whites until stiff but not brittle. Whisk the cream to the soft peak stage.

When the fruit mixture has begun to set, fold in the cream and then the egg whites and finally the liqueur. Turn the mixture into the prepared soufflé dish and level the top. Refrigerate until set.

To serve, carefully peel off the paper collar, using a knife dipped in hot water.

Decorate the top with piped cream, crystallised orange and lemon slices cut into wedges and pistachio nuts. Stand the soufflé dish on a dessert plate to serve.

HONEYDEW MELON SORBET

ILLUSTRATED ON PAGE 98

*This refreshing sorbet is ideal to serve after a curry or a rich main course. The sorbet
is presented in the melon shell and individual wedges are cut from it.*

No. of servings	6	12	24	48
ripe honeydew melon	1	2	4	8
caster sugar	175 g/6 oz	350 g/12 oz	700 g/1½ lb	1.4 kg/3 lb
lemon juice, about	3 tablespoons	6 tablespoons	180 ml/6 fl oz	360 ml/12 fl oz
egg whites	2	3	6	12

DECORATION *frosted mint leaves*

Cut the melon in half lengthwise, discard the pips
and scoop out the flesh. Put the flesh into a blender
with the sugar and lemon juice and whisk until the
sugar has dissolved. Pour into a freezing tray and
freeze until mushy. Meanwhile, cut each half of
the melon shell lengthwise into 3 wedges.

Line 2 plastic bowls with foil and put each half
shell into one of them, reforming it into its original
shape. Chill in the freezer. When the melon ice is
mushy, turn it into a bowl and whisk it up. Whisk
the egg white until stiff, but not brittle, and fold it
into the melon mixture. Pour it back into the
melon shells and freeze.

When serving, separate the wedges by cutting
through the water ice with a knife dipped in hot
water. Place the wedges on individual dessert
plates and decorate with frosted mint leaves.

Serve immediately as sorbets quickly melt.

ICED BERRY PARFAIT

*This delicious parfait can be made with strawberries, raspberries or loganberries,
either fresh or frozen, or canned in light syrup. If the fruit is canned in heavy syrup,
the parfait will be too sweet.*

No. of servings	6	12	24	48
strawberries, fresh frozen or canned	350 g/12 oz	625 g/1½ lb	1.3 kg/3 lb	2.7 kg/6 lb
egg whites, small	2	4	8	16
caster sugar	75 g/3 oz	150 g/6 oz	300 g/12 oz	625 g/1½ lb
water	3 tablespoons	6 tablespoons	180 ml/6 fl oz	350 ml/12 fl oz
lemon juice	1½ tablespoons	3 tablespoons	6 tablespoons	180 ml/6 fl oz
whipping cream	225 ml/8 fl oz	450 ml/¾ pint	900 ml/1½ pint	1.8 ml/3 pints

GARNISH *whole berries, fresh or frozen; piped cream*

If using canned fruit, strain off the juice and reserve. Sieve the fruit, measure the purée and make up to 225 ml/8 fl oz for 6 portions, 450 ml/16 fl oz for 12, 900 ml/1½ pints for 24, 1.8 ml/3 pints for 48, with juice from the tin. Whisk the egg whites to a stiff snow. Put the sugar and water in a thick saucepan over a moderate heat and stir until dissolved. Bring to a boil and cook rapidly without stirring until the syrup reaches 120 c, 250 f. Leave until it stops bubbling and pour slowly into the egg whites in a steady stream, stirring continuously with a wooden spoon. When all the syrup is in, continue to beat with an electric or hand mixer until thick and shiny and it stands in soft peaks. Stir in the fruit purée and lemon juice.

Whip the cream to the soft peak stage and gradually fold it into the mixture. Sharpen to taste with lemon juice. Pour the parfait for each six portions into a 900-ml/1½-pint mould or 6 individual shapes and freeze. To serve, take the large mould out of the freezer 1 hour before required, decorate with piped cream and whole fresh or frozen berries. Put into the refrigerator until serving. Individual moulds should be taken out of the freezer 15 minutes before serving.

Unless you have specialized catering equipment, it is advisable not to make more than 12 portions of the parfait mixture at a time.

Serve with crisp, plain petits fours or macaroons.

BASIC RECIPES

A really well made, delicately flavoured sauce can turn a fairly ordinary chop or fish fillet into a dinner party dish. In the same way an imaginative salad dressing can make a simple green salad a tasty accompaniment to cold meat or fish. In this chapter there are the basic recipes for sauces, dressings, pastries and sweet creams to serve with many of the dishes in this book.

SALAD DRESSINGS AND SAUCES

French Dressing (Sauce Vinaigrette)

The basic French dressing or Sauce vinaigrette is made with wine or cider vinegar, not the coarse malt vinegar used for pickling. Good quality salad oil is essential. Use olive or sunflower oil. French dressing and lemon dressing should both store well but should be re-whisked or shaken well before use.

To make	1 litre/2 pints
French mustard	2 teaspoons
salt	$\frac{1}{2}$ teaspoon
freshly ground black pepper	$\frac{1}{4}$ teaspoon
wine or cider vinegar	250 ml/$\frac{1}{2}$ pint
salad oil	750 ml/1$\frac{1}{2}$ pints

Mix the mustard, salt, pepper and vinegar and whisk until the salt has dissolved. Stir in the oil and whisk until the mixture has emulsified.

Lemon French Dressing

Use lemon juice instead of vinegar and make as you would French dressing. Chopped fresh tarragon and caster sugar can be added to taste.

Sauce Ravigote

You can use this dressing for artichokes and cold meat salads.

To make	1 litre/2 pints
shallots, finely chopped	30 g/1 oz
capers, finely chopped	30 g/1 oz
tarragon, chervil, chives parsley, finely chopped	30 g/1 oz
sauce vinaigrette (see left)	1 litre/1$\frac{3}{4}$ pints

Mix the shallots, capers and herbs together and whisk in the basic Sauce vinaigrette.

Robin Adair's Orange Salad Dressing

Serve this dressing with winter salads made from chopped chicory, apple, walnuts and watercress.

To make	500 ml/17 fl oz
small cloves garlic, crushed	4
French mustard	1 teaspoon
Worcestershire sauce	2 tablespoons
port	4 tablespoons
small oranges	4
Sauce vinaigrette	500 ml/17 fl oz
caster sugar	to taste

Mix together the garlic, mustard, Worcestershire sauce and port. Grate the rind off the oranges and squeeze out the juice. Add the rind and juice. Whisk in the Sauce vinaigrette. Sweeten to taste with caster sugar.

Gribiche Sauce

This is an excellent sauce for cold foods such as cold asparagus, artichokes, broccoli, cauliflower, fish, chicken, turkey and pheasant. It must be stored in the refrigerator, so it is not advisable to make it in very large quantities.

To make	600 ml/1 pint
hard-boiled eggs	3
egg yolks	4
French mustard	1 teaspoon
salt	$\frac{1}{4}$ teaspoon
freshly ground black pepper	$\frac{1}{2}$ teaspoon
good quality salad oil	600 ml/1 pint
gherkin, drained and minced	2 tablespoons
parsley, chopped	1 tablespoon
chives, chopped	1 tablespoon
tarragon vinegar	1 tablespoon
lemon juice	to taste

Separate and sieve the hard-boiled egg yolks. Chop the whites finely.

In a processor, mix the raw egg yolks with the mustard, salt and pepper and blend in the sieved hard-boiled yolks. Add the oil very gradually as for mayonnaise, keeping the machine running. Add a little vinegar if the sauce gets too thick.

Add the chopped gherkin, parsley and chives and the chopped hard-boiled egg whites. Adjust the seasoning and sharpen with the lemon juice.

Mayonnaise

To make	1 litre/$1\frac{3}{4}$ pints
eggs	6
French mustard	1 teaspoon
freshly ground black pepper	$\frac{1}{2}$ teaspoon
salt	1 teaspoon
cider or wine vinegar	65 ml/$2\frac{1}{2}$ fl oz
lemon juice	1 tablespoon

Put the eggs into a processor. Add the mustard, salt, pepper and vinegar and mix for 10 seconds. Pour the oil through the feed funnel in a steady stream. When made, the sauce should keep its shape when heaped on a spoon. Adjust the seasoning. If a thinner sauce is needed, add a little lemon juice or vinegar. If a thicker one is needed add 1 or 2 extra egg yolks.

Sauce Tartare

To make	1 litre/$1\frac{3}{4}$ pints
mayonnaise (page 182)	1 litre/$1\frac{3}{4}$ pints
shallots, finely chopped	25 g/1 oz
gherkin, finely chopped	25 g/1 oz
capers, finely chopped	50 g/2 oz
tarragon	15 g/$\frac{1}{2}$ oz
parsley	15 g/$\frac{1}{2}$ oz
seasoning	to taste

Stir all the ingredients into the mayonnaise. If the sauce is too sharp add a little extra sugar.

Sauce Rémoulade

ILLUSTRATED ON PAGE 128

To make	1 litre/$1\frac{3}{4}$ pints
mayonnaise (page 182)	1 litre/$1\frac{3}{4}$ pints
anchovy essence	1 tablespoon
capers, finely chopped	60 g/2 oz
gherkins, finely chopped	30 g/1 oz
Dijon mustard	2 teaspoons

Stir all the ingredients into the mayonnaise. The anchovy essence and mustard can be adjusted to taste.

Hollandaise Sauce

This is a versatile sauce that can be used for vegetables, fish and poultry.

There are two types of hollandaise sauce. The original recipe is flavoured with lemon juice, as in method I. In method II a reduction of vinegar and herbs is used. As hollandaise sauce is liable to separate if it is kept hot and it will solidify if chilled, it is advisable to make it in small quantities suitable for immediate use. If you add cream to the sauce you can serve it cold as mousseline sauce.

Method I

To make	500 ml/17 fl oz
egg yolks	4
lemon juice	2 tablespoons
water	2 tablespoons
butter, unsalted	400 g/14 oz
salt and white pepper	to taste

In a processor, whisk the egg yolks with the lemon juice, water and 1 tablespoon of the butter until well mixed. Keep the machine running. Melt the rest of the butter, take it off the heat and when it stops bubbling slowly pour it in through the filling tube of the processor. When the sauce has thickened, season it to taste, adding more lemon juice if required. Serve while still warm.

You can also make this sauce by hand. In which case you must place the bowl with the ingredients in it in a bain-marie or over a saucepan of boiling water and stir until thickened.

Hollandaise Sauce

Method II

To make	500 ml/17 fl oz
vinegar	25 ml/1 fl oz
salt and black pepper	to taste
egg yolks	4
butter, unsalted	400 g/14 oz
lemon juice	to taste

Reduce the vinegar and pepper to 2 tablespoons, strain and cool. Continue as in method I, but replacing the lemon juice by the reduced vinegar.

Béarnaise Sauce

This sauce is a perfect accompaniment to grilled fish or meat.

To make	500 ml/17 fl oz
shallots, finely chopped	25 g/1 oz
tarragon vinegar	25 ml/1 fl oz
freshly ground black pepper	to taste
water	1 tablespoon
egg yolks	4
butter, unsalted	400 g/14 oz
tarragon, chopped	1 tablespoon
chervil, chopped	1 tablespoon
lemon juice	to taste
salt and freshly ground black pepper	to taste

Put the shallots, tarragon vinegar and pepper into a saucepan and boil them until they are reduced to 1 tablespoon. Strain and add the water.

In the processor, whisk the reduced vinegar with the egg yolks until blended, melt the butter and with the machine running, slowly pour it through the filling tube. When the sauce has thickened add the chopped herbs and season to taste with lemon juice, salt and pepper. Serve while still warm.

Cumberland Sauce

This sauce goes very well with ham, pork, duck, goose or venison.

To make	500 ml/17 fl oz
redcurrant jelly	500 ml/17 fl oz
port	100 ml/4 fl oz
orange juice	100 ml/4 fl oz
lemon juice	50 ml/2 fl oz
blanched, shallots, chopped (optional)	25 g/1 oz
cornflour	2–3 teaspoons

GARNISH *juliennes of orange and lemon rind*

Remove the zest of 1 orange and ½ lemon in juliennes for the garnish before squeezing out the juice.

Melt the redcurrant jelly in a saucepan. Add the wine, fruit juice and shallots if used. Simmer for 3 minutes. If the sauce needs thickening, slake cornflour with a little cold water, add it to the sauce and simmer for 3 minutes until transparent.

Add the garnish and serve hot or cold.

Bread Sauce

Serve this sauce with hot or cold meats such as poultry, veal and game.

To make	500 ml/17 fl oz
milk	500 ml/17 fl oz
bay leaf	1
clove studded large onion	1
fresh white breadcrumbs	50 g/2 oz
seasoning	to taste
ground nutmeg	pinch
butter	50 g/2 oz

Simmer the milk with the bay leaf and the onion studded with whole cloves for about 15 minutes.

Remove the onion and the bayleaf and add the breadcrumbs. Mix thoroughly and simmer for 2–3 minutes. Do not boil. Add the seasoning and the nutmeg. Stir in the butter and adjust the consistency. Serve hot or cold.

NOTE: *For an extra creamy sauce, reduce the quantity of butter slightly and finish the sauce with 5 tablespoons of single cream.*

Espagnole Sauce

To make	1 litre/1¾ pints
MIREPOIX	
onion, peeled	250 g/8 oz
mushrooms	125 g/4 oz
celery	125 g/4 oz
carrot, peeled	250 g/8 oz
streaky bacon	125 g/4 oz
fat	125 g/4 oz
flour, about	125 g/4 oz
dry sherry	100 ml/3 fl oz
tomato juice	250 ml/9 fl oz
brown stock	600 ml/1 pint
mixed dried herbs	1 teaspoon
salt and black pepper	to taste
lemon juice	to taste

Chop the vegetables for the mirepoix. Take the rind off the bacon and chop it. Heat the fat and fry the vegetables and bacon in it until golden. Stir in enough flour to absorb the fat and fry, stirring, until caramel coloured. Stir in the sherry and cook brisky for 3 minutes. Add the herbs and tomato juice and stir in the stock. Season with salt and freshly ground black pepper and add lemon juice to taste. Cover and cook for 30 minutes or until the vegetables are tender. Adjust the seasoning.

If you need a smooth sauce, purée it in a blender or sieve it in a mouli-légumes.

Serve with dark poultry meat, beef, liver and kidneys.

Burgundy Sauce

Make this as you would Espagnole Sauce (see page 185) but use red wine instead of sherry, doubling the quantity and reducing the amount of stock accordingly.

Sauce Velouté

To make	1 litre/1¾ pints
butter or margarine	100 g/4 oz
flour	100 g/4 oz
white stock (page 32) (chicken, veal or fish)	1 litre/1¾ pints
bouquet garni	1
mushroom trimmings (as available)	

Melt the butter and over a gentle heat mix in the flour and cook, stirring steadily for a few minutes to make a smooth blond roux.

Add the stock gradually and when incorporated add the bouquet garni and the mushroom trimmings. Simmer for about 30 minutes.

Strain through a conical sieve. Cover to prevent a skin from forming and keep warm in a bain-marie.

Serve with white poultry, fish, shellfish, vegetables and hard-boiled eggs.

Bercy Sauce

ILLUSTRATED ON PAGE 97

This sauce is made with fish stock (see page 33) if it is to be served with fish dishes and with white meat stock (see page 32) for veal and lamb cutlets.

To make	450 ml/¾ pint
butter	50 g/2 oz
shallots, finely chopped	50 g/2 oz
white wine	250 ml/8 fl oz
white stock, fish or meat (pages 32–3)	450 ml/¾ pint
cream	100 ml/4 fl oz

Melt the butter and fry the shallots in it until transparent, but not coloured. Add the wine and stock and boil until reduced by half. Cream the flour and butter together to make the beurre manié (see below) and roll it into marble sized balls.

Add the pieces of beurre manié gradually to the simmering sauce and stir until it thickens to the right consistency.

Remove from the heat, stir in the cream and season to taste.

Beurre Manié

flour	50 g/2 oz
butter	50 g/2 oz
salt and freshly ground black pepper	to taste

PASTRY

Plain Shortcrust

This quantity will make two 18-cm/7-in flans which will divide into 8 portions. It can also be made into 6 individual flans or 12 tartlets.

Yields	400 g/12 oz
plain flour	225 g/8 oz
salt	$\frac{1}{4}$ teaspoon
margarine or lard or half and half	100 g/4 oz
cold water	to mix

Sift flour and salt in a mixing bowl. Rub in the fat lightly until the mixture resembles breadcrumbs. Mix in enough cold water to make a stiff, not sticky dough. Knead lightly into a ball and shape.

Rich Shortcrust

This quantity will make two 20-cm/8-in flans which will divide into 12 portions.

Yields	450 g/14 oz
plain flour	225 g/8 oz
salt	$\frac{1}{4}$ teaspoon
butter and lard (half and half)	100 g/4 oz
egg yolk	1–2
cold water	to mix

Sift the flour and mix in the fat until the mixture resembles breadcrumbs. Mix 2 tablespoons of water with the beaten egg yolks. Stir into the flour mixture, adding enough water to make a soft, not sticky dough. Knead lightly into a ball, cover and leave to rest for at least 30 minutes. Shape and roll out to .5 cm/$\frac{1}{4}$ in thickness.

Rough Puff Pastry

This is enough pastry for 1 fish or meat pie and will serve 6. However for a Russian fish pie you will need more pastry (see page 68).

Yields	450 g/14 oz
plain flour	225 g/8 oz
salt	$\frac{1}{4}$ teaspoon
butter and lard (half and half)	175 g/6 oz
lemon juice	1 teaspoon
cold water	to mix

Sift the flour and the salt into a mixing bowl. Cut the fat into walnut sized cubes and toss lightly in the flour. Add the lemon juice to the water and mix into the flour to make a soft, not sticky dough. Gather into a ball. Shape into a rectangle on a floured board and roll with short, jerky rolls into a rectangle about 1 cm/$\frac{1}{2}$ in thick. Mark the pastry into three, fold up the bottom third, incorporating as much air as possible. Fold the top third over and seal the edges with the rolling pin. Give the pastry a quarter turn and roll it out into a rectangle again.

Repeat the folding, sealing, turning and rolling 4 times or until no fatty streaks remain. Chill well before using.

PASTRY FREEZING NOTE: *Pastry will freeze, defrost and reheat very successfully. If you need cold, cooked pastry use puff or flaky pastry.*

SWEET SAUCES

Chocolate Cream Sauce

Yields about	900 ml/1½ pints
plain block chocolate	450 g/1 lb
golden syrup	225 g/8 oz
single cream	300 ml/½ pint
rum or Tia Maria (optional)	to taste

Break up the chocolate and put it in a bowl over a pan of hot water and heat. Make sure that the water does not touch the base of the bowl. Add the syrup and stir until thoroughly blended. Remove the bowl from the heat and slowly stir in the cream. Flavour to taste with rum or Tia Maria. Serve with rich chocolate pudding (see page 171) or profiteroles or ice cream.

Orange Foam Sauce

Yields	1.1 litres/2 pints
unsalted butter	250 g/9 oz
orange, grated rind and juice	5
flour	75 g/3 oz
caster sugar	125 g/4½ oz
eggs, separated	5
water, about	750 ml/1¼ pints
lemon juice	to taste

Cream the butter with the grated orange rind and gradually beat in the flour and sugar mixed together. Beat in the egg yolks and enough water to make the juice up to 1.1 litres/2 pints. If the mixture curdles at this stage, it will, however, blend smoothly as it cooks. Stir the sauce over a gentle heat until it thickens and the flour is thoroughly cooked. If necessary add a little water to keep the sauce at a pouring consistency. Beat the egg whites until stiff, but not brittle. Shortly before serving, fold them into the sauce. Sharpen the sauce to taste with lemon juice. Serve with Orange cup pudding (see page 177) and other puddings usually served with custard.

CREAMS

Crème Chantilly

(Chantilly Cream)

This light, slightly sweetened cream is a favourite accompaniment to both hot and cold puddings.

Yields	530 ml/19 fl oz
cream, double	450 ml/16 fl oz
cream, single	80 ml/3 fl oz
vanilla essence, a few drops	2
egg white, beaten (optional)	2

Beat the creams together and stir in the vanilla essence. The egg white will give the cream a fluffy texture.

CRÈME PÂTISSIÈRE (PASTRY CREAM)

This cream can be used in a Gâteau St Honoré and for filling profiteroles.

Yields	300 ml/½ pint	600 ml/1 pint	1.2 ml/2 pints	2.4 ml/4 pints
egg yolks	2	4	8	16
egg white	1	2	4	8
caster sugar	50 g/2 oz	100 g/4 oz	225 g/8 oz	450 g/1 lb
plain flour, sieved	25 g/1 oz	50 g/2 oz	100 g/4 oz	225 g/8 oz
milk	300 ml/½ pint	600 ml/1 pint	1.2 ml/2 pints	2.4 ml/4 pints

FLAVOURING *vanilla or lemon juice or sweet sherry or liqueur or rum, to taste*

Whisk the eggs and sugar together until white and creamy, gradually stir in the flour and then the milk. Pour into a saucepan and stirring steadily throughout, bring to the boil and simmer gently for 3–5 minutes to cook the flour thoroughly. Add the flavouring and spread in a dish to cool. Stir occasionally to prevent a skin from forming.

INDEX